CONTROVERSY!

Poverty in America: Cause or Effect?

Joan Axelrod-Contrada

Marshall Cavendish
Benchmark
New York

With thanks to Ezra Rosser, assistant professor of law at American University Washington College of Law in Washington, D.C., for his expert review of this manuscript.

Marshall Cavendish Benchmark
99 White Plains Road
Tarrytown, NY 10591
www.marshallcavendish.us

Cover: A homeless person sleeps wrapped in plastic to saty warm.

All websites were available and accurate when this book was sent to press.

Library of Congress CIP Data
Axelrod-Contrada, Joan.
Poverty in America : cause or effect? / by Joan Axelrod-Contrada.
p. cm. — (Controversy!)
Includes bibliographical references and index.
ISBN 978-0-7614-4236-3
1. Poverty—United States. 2. Poor--United States. I. Title.
HC110.P6A92 2010
339.4'60973—dc22
2008050185

Publisher: Michelle Bisson
Art Director: Anahid Hamparian
Series Designer: Alicia Mikles

Photo research by Lindsay Aveilhe and Linda Sykes Picture Research, Inc., Hilton Head, SC

Cover photo: Bettmann/Corbis
The photographs in this book are used by permission and through the courtesy of:
Bettmann/Corbis: 15; Reuters/Corbis: 4; The Granger Collection: 10; Hulton Archive/Getty Images: 13; Mario Tama/Getty Images: 19; Ed Kashi/Corbis: 21; David McNew/Getty Images: 24; Rick Wilking/Reuters/Corbids: 32; Alison Wright/Corbis: 34; Ariel Skelley/Corbis: 38; AP Images: 48, 58, 62; Emmanuel/AFP/Getty Images: 54; Nicole Bengiveno/ New York Times/Redux: 66; David McNew/Getty Images: 69; Joe Readle/Getty Images: 78; Ted Soqui/Corbis: 82; Mark Richards/PhotoEdit, Inc.: 85; Tannen Maury/epa/Corbis: 88; Karen Kasmauski/Corbis: 94; John Nordell/ Christian Science Monitor/Getty Images: 97.

Printed in Malaysia
1 3 5 6 4 2

Contents

Introduction

ON A TYPICAL DAY, MILLIONS OF AMERICANS STRUGGLE in the dark corners of the land of plenty.

One out of eight falls below the official poverty line set by the U.S. government. Many more live in that often overlooked land of the "near poor"—not poor enough to qualify for government benefits, but too poor to live a comfortable middle-class existence.

Scholars use the terms *absolute* and *relative* to describe two kinds of deprivation associated with poverty. While *absolute poverty* refers to a state in which one's very survival is threatened by the lack of resources, *relative poverty* takes into account a person's financial situation compared to the average income and lifestyle enjoyed by the rest of that society.

Economist Adam Smith offered the example of the linen shirt to illustrate his concept of relative poverty. In his 1776 book, *The Wealth of Nations*, Smith maintained that, while the linen shirt did not qualify as a necessity of life, it was an item "indecent for creditable people, even of the lowest order to be without." Social norms varied by time and place. "The Greeks and Romans lived, I suppose, very comfortably, though they had no linen. But in the present times, through the greater part of Europe, a creditable day-laborer would be ashamed to appear in public without a linen shirt,

The United States is a land of contradictions: so much for same, so little for too many. Here, a homeless family eats their takeout Thanksgiving meal in view of the U.S. Capitol.

the want of which would be supposed to denote that disgraceful degree of poverty, which, it is presumed, no body can well fall into without extreme bad conduct."

Along similar lines, few low-income Americans—the homeless are a notable exception—live in the kind of absolute poverty characteristic of the developing world. Most people in the United States enjoy amenities such as running water, electricity, and TV, which people in Bangladesh or Kenya might consider luxuries. But being poor in a rich land takes its own kind of toll. People with limited resources lack the power and choices of those above them on the social and economic ladder.

While poverty in America cuts across racial lines, it disproportionately affects blacks, Hispanics, and American Indians. Teen pregnancy and single-parent families also increase the risk of poverty. Statistics, however, tell only part of the story. Behind the numbers are real people struggling with the stress of not having enough. Something has to go. Should it be food, or heat? A car, or health care? Quality child care, or housing?

Invariably, one problem complicates another. The child who goes to bed hungry wakes up unable to concentrate in school, which in turn increases the risk of dropping out, getting low-wage work, and being unable to afford a car or decent housing. Everything affects something else because there's no financial cushion. When emergencies strike, debts pile up.

Take the case of Willie Goodell. Profiled by author David K. Shipler in *The Working Poor: Invisible in America*, Willie, a roofer in his twenties, incurred ten thousand dollars in medical bills. His teeth were decaying, but, because he could not afford health insurance, he went to the emergency room whenever he needed help. Because he could not pay his emergency-room bills, Willie ruined his credit rating. Meanwhile, he continued to smoke cigarettes. Sacrificing this small comfort seemed like more than he could bear.

Who's to blame for Willie's plight? Willie himself or society? Policy makers have long differed in their answers to such questions. While conservatives have emphasized the role of individual responsibility, liberals have pointed to the need for better economic and social supports. The nation's response to poverty—from poorhouses to welfare reform—has changed with the times.

For generations, segregation limited the opportunites of African Americans. Even though civil rights legislation eliminated legal discrimination, inequalities remain. Blacks, for instance, are less likely than whites to inherit wealth.

Increasingly experts use the term *social capital* to describe the myriad ways in which social interactions matter. For instance, researchers have found that people from disadvantaged communities lack access to the social networks that bolster one's chances for educational and career success.

Although America prides itself on being a land of opportunity, the notion that anyone who is willing and able can "pull themselves up by their bootstraps" may be more myth than reality. The poor in the United States experience less economic mobility than their counterparts in other developed nations. For sons in the United States, the chance of having the same low earnings as their fathers is 42.2 percent, compared to less than 30 percent in Denmark, Finland, Norway, and Sweden. In Scandinavian countries, universal health care and greater child-care subsidies may help less advantaged members of society better reach their economic potential. The income gap between the rich and poor in the United States is much wider, with the top 20 percent of U.S. households receiving over half of all income, while the bottom 20 percent receives only about 3 percent of total income.

In recent years, poverty increasingly has spread into the suburbs. With the middle class besieged by stagnant wages, record layoffs, and rising expenses, the rungs on the ladder of opportunity have become increasingly shaky. In urban and rural communities, many people lead lives cut off from the American mainstream, relegated to areas of high joblessness and poor schools.

Meanwhile, workers in the United States have been hit hard by globalization and the loosening of labor regulations. Once-secure jobs in the manufacturing sector increasingly are being shipped out to low-wage workers overseas. Employees who try to organize unions to better their conditions often face an uphill battle marked by employers' virulent antilabor campaigns. As welfare reform sends a growing number of former recipients into the workforce, questions swirl about the kinds of jobs they'll find.

Can the rapidly growing service sector provide new hope for the future? If so, how can currently low-paying jobs, such as flipping burgers and changing bedpans, offer a living wage? What can be done to repair the holes in the safety net so everyone has access to quality health coverage, child care, education, and housing?

Author Robert David Rank uses the metaphor of a game of musical chairs to discuss strategies to bring more seats to America's table of plenty. Because the roots of poverty reach deep, no one solution will magically eliminate the blight. Instead, experts recommend a broad-based approach. Many experts argue that poverty-related problems, such as crime and poor health, cost taxpayers money that could be better spent on programs to eliminate poverty. A public mandate to end poverty would repair the frayed fabric of the American Dream.

Meanwhile, a new federal administration has signed into law a bill designed to stimulate the economy while it expands its safety net to the nation's poor and near-poor. As both the domestic and world economies remained in recession in early 2009, the questions became even more pressing.

1 Historical Overview

AMERICA BECKONED.

It was the Land of Opportunity, the place where people could come for a better life. Conditions in seventeenth-century England had taken a turn for the worse. The enclosure system cost many small farmers their common grazing lands, driving them into the cities to look for work. The landless poor who flocked to London in the late 1600s found a city full of drunkards, beggars, and thieves. Three out of five boys died before they reached the age of sixteen. Many people spent what little money they had on alcohol, rather than food, to dull the pain of their squalid lives.

The English government wanted to unload its convicts and surplus poor on America. Broadsides (flyers) for America portrayed the new land in glowing terms. However, few of England's poor had the money or the interest in journeying across the stormy Atlantic to settle in an unknown land.

Finally, the Virginia Company, an organization of merchants and wealthy men in England chartered by King James I to settle the New World, offered a possible solution. The new colony desperately needed laborers. The company would pay the costs of transportation to America in return for the promise of workers. Newcomers would receive free land at the end of their service. Other merchants followed suit, hiring subcontractors to get prospective colonists to sign "indentures" agreeing to work a certain number of years in exchange for transportation to America. Unscrupulous

SELLING WIVES TO THE PLANTERS.

Many men were sent to the British colony of Jamestown, Virginia, as indentured servants. Many women were twice indentured: first sent as servants, then married off to male settlers, often traded for tobacco or other desired goods.

agents plied prospective colonists with drink to get them to sign away their rights.

About half of all white immigrants to the English colonies during the seventeenth century were convicts or indentured servants. For some of these contract laborers, the risk paid off. They finished their period of service and became free farmers or workers. Others, however, found harsh toil and broken promises. Those who spent their time "idly or unprofitably" could be sent to hard labor or whipped.

In the first half of the eighteenth century, the system of white indentured servitude tapered off. Plantation owners found black slaves from Africa to be a better bargain. These new slaves could be purchased to work until they died.

The "Deserving Poor" vs. "Paupers"

"A penny saved is a penny earned," Benjamin Franklin said in his famous maxim, expressing the popular wisdom of his day. Hard work kept people on the right path. Laziness bred poverty. Franklin disapproved of government welfare programs because he believed they took away "all inducements to industry, frugality, and sobriety."

Every Sunday ministers preached about the sins of idleness. Still, they knew that not everyone could work. Paupers were whipped, auctioned off, and sent to workhouses. Charities and government relief, meanwhile, sprang up to serve those considered deserving of help. The ministers lauded charity for the sick, the infirm, orphans, widows, and others in need.

Colonists drew a firm line between the "deserving" and the "undeserving" poor. While they gave generously to those deemed unable to help themselves, they showed considerably less sympathy for the able-bodied poor they regarded as "paupers." As one theorist put it: "Pauperism is the consequence of wilful error, of shameful indolence, of vicious habits." An increase of pauperism in the early 1800s led to a new search for answers. Contemporary experts saw a strong link between poverty and heavy drinking. In Massachusetts, for instance, the Quincy report concluded: "That of all the causes of pauperism, intemperance, in the use of spirituous liquors is the most powerful and universal."

Many communities established poorhouses (also called "almshouses" and "poor farms"). At first, the poorhouses seemed like a sensible alternative to doling out relief that could be abused by able-bodied vagrants. The institutions opened with the promise of reforming the morally flawed. Supervisors would ban both idleness and alcohol. Inmates would be kept busy farming their own food, weaving, and making tools.

However, the poorhouses failed to live up to their initial promise. Outdoor work tapered off in the winter. With operating costs kept low to act as a deterrent, poorhouses degenerated into institutions of mismanagement and squalor. Inmates stole liquor from the managers' private stock or bought it from corrupt employees. One report complained that the almshouse had become "a winter resort for tramps. . . a place where the drunkard and the prostitute" recuperated "between debauches."

By the 1850s, criticism of the workhouses led to the creation of new private charities and local government relief. The Civil War brought the end of slavery for African Americans in 1865, but they continued to find limited economic opportunities. Meanwhile, the gap between the rich and the poor grew. New immigrants from Eastern Europe clustered in tenements in the great cities. Abandoned children ran wild in these breeding grounds of crime, disease, and despair.

The Progressive Era

Jane Addams and other reformers of the Progressive Era questioned the notion that poverty was synonymous with vice and laziness. Instead of blaming poverty on the individual, they pointed to social and economic conditions responsible for the growing gap between rich and poor.

A pioneer in the new field of social work, Addams was born September 6, 1860. She grew up the daughter of a progressive-minded Illinois legislator and businessman who was a strong supporter of Abraham Lincoln. Even as a young child, Addams was shocked by the "horrid little houses" and garbage-strewn streets of Chicago. She identified with the victims of society because she, herself, felt like a misfit: a pigeon-toed little girl who suffered from a curvature of the spine.

After touring a mission for the poor in the slums of London, Addams founded Hull House in Chicago in 1889, launching the settlement-house movement in America. Instead of merely visiting the poor like traditional charity workers, she lived among

Jane Addams was an early reformer who believed that education was the road out of poverty. Here, an instructor at Hull House teaches chemistry to young women who took part in a program that trained them to become nurses.

them, bridging the gap between the classes. Hull House provided meaningful careers for a new generation of college-educated young women who became settlement workers. A proponent of women's suffrage, Addams viewed women as "civic housekeepers."

She and other reformers sponsored legislation to abolish child labor, establish juvenile courts, limit the hours of working women, and make school attendance mandatory. In 1912, the Progressive Party, headed by Theodore Roosevelt, supported many of these reforms as part of its platform.

However, after Addams failed to support World War I (1914–1918), her popularity faded. Reforms that seemed "praiseworthy before the war," said Addams, became "suspect" after it. With Addams discredited because she was seen as a radical, social workers saw less of a need to live in the neighborhoods they served. Calls for government involvement to supplement private charity fell on deaf ears.

Poverty, however, persisted. Farmers suffered a decade-long depression in the 1920s, and low-skilled workers often found themselves out of work or with wages too low to support their families.

Still, most people hailed the Roaring Twenties as a time of great prosperity. Sales of consumer goods boomed. The horse and buggy gave way to the automobile. Many people bought on credit and gambled on the stock market. Little did they know that the economic bubble was about to burst.

The Great Depression

On Black Tuesday, October 29, 1929, the stock market crashed, triggering the worst depression in U.S. history. Banks and businesses closed down. President Herbert Hoover, a strong believer in rugged individualism, underestimated the seriousness of the crisis. Calling the Depression a "temporary halt in the prosperity of a great people," he rejected calls for the federal government to provide relief to the 15 million Americans affected (one-quarter of the workforce). Instead, he set forth a program of government aid to businesses. His efforts accomplished little.

Across the nation, out-of-work bankers stood in bread lines with unemployed laborers. The Great Depression deeply wounded the psyche of Americans who had long associated their self-worth with their work. Many unemployed fathers left home, ashamed of being unable to support their loved ones. Children, too, took off, so as not to burden their families.

With no jobs to support themselves, people lost their homes. The homeless built shacks of cardboard, scrap metal, packing boxes, and tar paper, which they called "Hoovervilles" out of bitterness toward the president's failed policies. Local aid and private charity had nowhere near the resources to deal with the needs of the impoverished.

In 1932, the American people voted for change by electing Franklin Delano Roosevelt president in a landslide victory. Presi-

The Great Depression in the United States was a time when the poor stood in line outside churches for handouts of bread and coffee. Though religious organizations still have food banks, the government took a greater hand in helping the poor as a result of the suffering of that time.

dent Roosevelt quickly set in motion his plan for a New Deal. Heeding the call of "jobs not the dole," Congress approved a sweeping Works Progress Administration (WPA), which put millions of people to work in both blue-collar and white-collar jobs. In addition, Congress passed the Social Security Act, establishing a payroll tax to provide benefits for retirees and others in need. The act created a welfare program known as Aid to Dependent Children. President Roosevelt signed the Social Security Act on August 14, 1935.

The Great Depression ended with the start of World War II and the creation of military-related jobs. The late 1940s and 1950s ushered in another era of prosperity bolstered by the passage of the G.I. Bill in 1944. Anyone who had served in the military could take advantage of government assistance for college tuition and a home mortgage. In the 1950s, the suburbs grew.

Not everyone, however, benefited from the new prosperity. In 1962, the publication of Michael Harrington's groundbreaking book, *The Other America*, focused new attention on poverty in the land of plenty.

The War on Poverty

In a dramatic address to Congress on March 16, 1964, President Lyndon B. Johnson declared a war on poverty.

> Today we are asked to declare war on a domestic enemy which threatens the strength of our nation and the welfare of our people. If we now move forward against the enemy—if we can bring to the challenges of peace the same determination and strength which has brought us victory in war—then this day and this Congress will have won a secure and honorable place in the history of the nation and the enduring gratitude of generations of Americans yet to come.

President Johnson's initiative set in motion a series of bills and acts, creating programs such as Head Start, food stamps, work study, Medicare, and Medicaid, all of which still exist today. New provisions strengthened Social Security, reducing poverty among the elderly. The civil rights movement of the 1960s brought new legislation to end racial discrimination. But, as urban riots and the Vietnam War grabbed headlines, support for LBJ's Great Society faded. Because of a lack of funding, the programs proved to be not so much a "war" on poverty as a "skirmish."

In 1967, presidential candidate Robert F. Kennedy saw with

his own eyes how poor people lived. Touring the Mississippi Delta, he stopped to chat with impoverished black children who lived in windowless shacks. Americans reacted with shock upon seeing TV images of poor children with distended bellies from malnutrition. Kennedy's supporters suffered a major blow when he was assassinated shortly after midnight on June 5, 1968. Old problems lingered, and new issues surfaced.

In his book, *Losing Ground: American Social Policy 1950–1980*, author Charles Murray described how an era of unprecedented social reform gave rise to unexpected consequences. Old welfare policies regarded by many critics as overly harsh gave way to more flexible policies, prompting a 125 percent increase in caseloads between 1965 and 1970. Murray argued that the new welfare regulations did a disservice to the poor by making it profitable to make short-term choices that would be destructive in the long run. Murray used the example of "Harold and Phyllis," a hypothetical young couple of unspecified race, to illustrate how people's behavior changed in response to shifts in government policy.

In Murray's scenario, Harold and Phyllis have just graduated from an average public school in an average American city when Phyllis becomes pregnant. In 1960, harsh regulations against having "a man in the house" and supplementing her income would have discouraged Phyllis from going on welfare. The couple probably would have gotten married and scraped by on their own earnings. If Harold was lucky, he'd move up from his job operating the steam-presses in a laundry to driving the company's delivery truck to finding a unionized truck-driving job. By 1970, the rules had changed, and the new regulations made it logical for Phyllis to go on welfare and not get married. Harold probably would work only sporadically in the laundry, finding little reason to search for something better.

As time went on, stereotypes of lazy black welfare recipients reduced public sympathy for the poor. President Ronald Reagan, for instance, talked about a "welfare queen" in Chicago with a mink coat and a Cadillac. When reporters searched for the real welfare recipient behind the story, they found that the woman accused of using eighty names and bilking the government out of more than $150,000 actually had used two different aliases to collect $8,000.

Conservatives such as Reagan were not the only ones who saw problems with the welfare system. As the economy faltered, questions swirled about the government's aid to the poor. Had the expansion of the Aid to Families with Dependent Children program (a successor to the Aid to Dependent Children program created in 1935) made it too easy for people to just live off the government? Was the government creating a new culture of welfare dependency?

Ending "Welfare as We Know It"

In 1992, Bill Clinton campaigned for the presidency on a promise to "end welfare as we know it." Once in office, President Clinton proposed a plan to replace welfare with work, bolstered by supportive services. Congress modified his plan to trim costs. In 1996, President Clinton signed the Personal Responsibility and Work Opportunity Reconciliation Act (PRWORA). This measure replaced Aid to Families with Dependent Children (AFDC) with Temporary Aid to Needy Families (TANF). The new program, which included an education and training component, set temporary limits and a five-year lifetime cap on welfare assistance. States could exclude certain groups (such as parents of children under a year old and disabled adults) from work requirements.

Has the welfare reform act of 1996 accomplished its goal of transforming "the culture of poverty"? Experts say the results have been mixed. While employment has risen, many leave welfare to work in low-wage jobs. Increasingly, jobs have moved to the suburbs, creating problems of accessibility for urban residents.

In 2005, Hurricane Katrina focused new awareness on the

The poor were hardest hit by Hurricane Katrina. Many lost their homes in the devastating storm only to find that available rentals had both dwindled and almost doubled in price. Some, as shown here, ended up living under highways.

problems of the impoverished living on the margins of society. The majority of those trapped in New Orleans could not escape because they had no cars, no surplus money, and no place to go. Hurricane Katrina focused new attention on the problems of racial isolation and highly concentrated poverty.

Years later, the plight of the poor persists. The 2006 reauthorization of PRWORA required states to impose stricter work requirements. The new regulations raised the work-participation rates that states must meet from 50 percent of families with an adult receiving TANF assistance to 70 percent of such families by 2010. Throughout U.S. history, policy makers have struggled to balance personal responsibility with compassion. That struggle continues.

2 Broke in America

ALLISON REMEMBERS EXACTLY WHEN SHE REALIZED her family was poor.

She was sitting at her desk in sixth grade, looking at the calculations on the blackboard. Her teacher had just told the class that some people in America live in the upper class, others in the middle class, and still others in poverty.

"I counted the kids in my family, looked at her figures and came to the shocking realization that my family lives at poverty level," Allison told *Teen People*. "I couldn't have a lot of stuff I wanted, but I never thought about it that way before."

Like Allison, approximately 37 million Americans—one in eight—live below the poverty level set by the United States government. The poverty line in 2008 was $21,200 for a family of four. Poverty cuts across all racial and ethnic lines, although some groups have higher rates than others. Here's a statistical snapshot of who lives below the official poverty line:

- 12.6 percent of all Americans
- 8.3 percent of non-Hispanic whites
- 24.9 percent of blacks
- 21.8 percent of Hispanics
- 11.1 percent of Asians
- 25.3 percent of American Indians and Alaskan Natives

Some experts believe that the U.S. government sets its poverty line too low. For one thing, fixed expenses, such as rent, have

There are lots of ways to go broke in America, but a common way in recent years is to lack health insurance. Sheila Wessenberg panhandles for spare change along Highway 183 near Dallas, Texas, to try to find help for the medical bills resulting from her breast cancer treatment. Her husband lost his job—and with it, his six-figure income and health insurance.

increased since the government developed its formula in 1964. For another, the government's calculations fail to account for debt such as credit-card balances and college loans. Each month, debt eats up a substantial chunk of family income. Since 1949, total debt as a percentage of disposable income has increased nearly fourfold, according to the Brookings Institution. Finally, many people live on the fringes of poverty. They make too much money to qualify for government assistance but not enough to get by.

Poverty hits people in the psyche as well as the wallet. Often being broke makes people feel broken. The belief that anyone who works hard can make it in America stings those who don't have enough money to pay the bills. Life doesn't seem fair. Many in poverty feel like they're playing a game without enough chips to win.

Being poor in America is different from living in poverty in the developing world. Someone from Somalia or Bangladesh might view the running water, central heating, TVs, and cars of the poor in America with envy. However, being poor in a land of plenty poses special challenges. People want what they see around them. In his book *The Working Poor: Invisible in America*, author David Shipler writes that the skills of surviving in poverty that people in poor countries develop by necessity have largely been lost in America.

"Visit a slum in Hanoi and you will find children inventing games with bottles and sticks and the rusty rims of bicycle wheels," Shipler writes. "Go to a slum in Los Angeles and you will find children dependent on plastic toys and video games."

Food Insecurity

Few Americans exhibit the signs of extreme hunger—skeletal frames and distended bellies—common in the developing world. In America, hunger takes a more subtle form. Often, it creeps up on people. Many of those who qualify for government assistance use up their food stamps before the end of the month because of the high cost of groceries. Others make too much to qualify for food stamps but not enough to pay their bills *and* put food on the table. Both groups turn to charitable organizations that are having trouble keeping up with the growing demand for food. Researchers call the condition of being unable to buy enough groceries to last the month "food insecurity."

Because so few supermarket chains remain in the inner cities, many poor urban families are forced to rely on expensive mom-and-pop stores. Snacks and fast foods abound in these neighborhoods. Ironically some people are both obese and food insecure.

Gladys, a retiree in Seattle, Washington, spent 70 percent of her income on rent. After paying her bills, she had little money left for food. Like many senior citizens, she had health problems that required a special diet. But she didn't have a car. Without access to transportation, she couldn't get to the big supermarkets that offered the best prices and selections. Instead, she shopped at a little convenience store in her neighborhood.

"I can get very little with my money there," she said. "Most of the time I can't eat what I get at the food bank because my doctor wants me to follow a very strict diet. I have very high blood pressure and I'm also battling cancer, so I am supposed to eat a lot of vegetables and fruit. Those are very expensive and I am able to buy them very rarely."

Social Class

Experts use the term *class* to describe groups of people of similar economic and social position. Class is commonly described in terms of four criteria:

- Education
- Income
- Occupation
- Wealth

At first, a person's class is his or her parents' class. It's like everyone is dealt a hand of cards at birth—one from each suit: education, income, occupation, and health—but, later, players may pick up new hands of their own. Bill Clinton, for instance, began with low cards but emerged a winner thanks to a college education and a Rhodes scholarship.

In some ways, class differences have blurred over the years. "The old system of hereditary barriers and clubby barriers has pretty much vanished," said Eric Wanner, president of the Russell Sage Foundation, a social science research group in New York City. These days, it's harder than in the past to gauge class through material possessions, because factories in China and elsewhere churn out low-priced consumer goods. Discount stores sell low-priced imitations of designer clothes and home furnishings.

However, in other ways, class divisions have deepened in recent years. The gap between the rich and poor has widened: the after-tax income of the top one percent of American households jumped 139 percent between 1979 and 2001, compared to just 17

More and more union jobs—which provide a living wage and medical and other benefits—have been disappearing, with employers now taking away the benefits union organizers labored to earn for their members. Janitor Fidelina Escobar went on a three-day fast in support of fellow workers whom her employers had locked out of their jobs in an attempt to break their union.

percent for the middle fifth and only 9 percent for the poor. Class plays a big role in determining who gets into which four-year college. The proportion of students from upper-income families has grown, not shrunk, at 250 of the most selective colleges in the country.

Class differences also play an increased role in health, with Americans at the top of the class ladder living longer and maintaining better health than those at the bottom. Family structure differs considerably by class, as well, with the educated and affluent more likely to have children while married. Because privileged couples typically also have fewer children, they're in a superior position to invest in them. Finally, more than in the past, the affluent are choosing to live apart from everyone else in gated communities and exurban mansions.

Although African Americans have moved into the middle and

upper classes, race continues to shape their experiences. They're typically first-generation middle class and so, unlike whites, lack the accumulated wealth of previous generations. Blacks also are much more likely than whites to live near poor segregated areas.

Rising Up the Ladder

For generations, jobs in manufacturing have provided a stepping-stone from poverty into the ranks of the middle class. However, because many of these positions have been outsourced to lower-wage workers overseas, the working poor in the United States increasingly are toiling in service-sector positions in restaurants and stores, or in janitorial jobs.

For immigrants like Juan Manuel Peralta, the climb out of poverty can be particularly difficult. Peralta left Mexico at the age of nineteen to join his uncle in New York City. He expected to work hard and rise out of poverty. But, fifteen years later, that has yet to happen.

An illegal immigrant, he bounced from one restaurant job to another, married at the age of twenty-five, started a family, and eventually landed a job in the kitchen at 3 Guys, an upscale Greek restaurant in New York City. However, a combination of personal factors and work-related challenges held him back. Peralta's schedule at 3 Guys changed from week to week, making it impossible to count on a secure salary. Also, he sent part of his earnings back home to Mexico. Admittedly, he squandered some of the rest of his money on vices such as lottery tickets.

At 3 Guys, Peralta acquired a reputation as a hothead because he sometimes argued with waiters. Tensions flared between the predominantly Greek waiters and the lower-paid Mexican kitchen workers. Only one Mexican, who happened to look Greek, had been promoted to the position of waiter. After Peralta and other Mexicans brought their grievances to the Restaurant Opportunities Center, a workers' rights group, the owners promised to promote a

Mexican worker to waiter within a month. By the time the owners promoted a Mexican busboy to the position of waiter ten months later, Peralta had been fired (he denied his boss's contention that he was not a good worker).

After his stint at 3 Guys, Peralta went to work as a grill cook at a diner in Queens. His schedule, though, kept changing, and he found himself arguing with the Greek owner. One of those disagreements prompted him to leave and get a new job. Despite his setbacks, Peralta is earning more money in the United States than he would be in Mexico. However, he's not making enough to move out of poverty. His experiences show how difficult it can be to find upward mobility.

"The Missing Class"

Valerie Rushing moved up from poverty to the next rung on the socioeconomic ladder. After years of working low-wage jobs, the thirty-three-year-old African-American single mother landed a $13.68-an-hour janitorial job with the Long Island Rail Road. Her new position (complete with full benefits) helped her leave behind her old life of minimum-wage jobs as a child-care worker, shoe-store employee, and fast-food cashier.

Her story, profiled by authors Katherine S. Newman and Victor Tan Chen in their highly acclaimed book, *The Missing Class: Portraits of the Near Poor in America*, illustrates how difficult it can be for the near-poor to hold onto their hard-won victories. Newman and Chen coined the term "the missing class" to describe the 57 million people who live in households that earn roughly $20,000 to $40,000 a year. Although the 37 million officially poor Americans are profiled every census year, the near-poor are rarely on the nation's radar screen. Newman and Chen wrote their book to shine the spotlight on these Americans who generally earn too much to qualify for government assistance.

Rushing supported two children—her daughter Akeelah and

Immigrants and the American Dream

Twenty-year-old Manuel Espinoza-Vazquez faced the possibility of deportation after making an improper right turn.

When the police officer asked for his license, Espinoza-Vazquez produced a Mexican ID. The officer transported Espinoza-Vazquez, a student at Arizona State University, to the Immigration and Customs Enforcement Office in Phoenix, Arizona. "I'm scared . . . and my little sister cries," Espinoza-Vazquez told the *Arizona Republic*. "I just want to graduate."

His case points to the controversies around immigration in the United States. Supporters of broad-based rights for immigrants maintain that they do the hard work most native-born Americans don't want to do. Critics of such policies, on the other hand, point to the strain immigration puts on taxpayer-funded services. The Center for Immigration Studies reports that the nation's immigrant population (both legal and illegal) are more likely to be poor and to use welfare programs than native-born Americans, adding that:

- Immigrants account for one in eight U.S. residents;
- Nearly one in three immigrants is an illegal alien;
- The poverty rate for immigrants and their children is 17 percent, nearly 40 percent higher than the rate for natives and their children;
- The proportion of immigrant-headed households using at least one major welfare program is 33 percent, compared to 19 percent for households of native-born Americans;

- Immigration accounts for virtually all of the national increase in public school enrollment over the last two years.

While new immigrants lack the education levels of native-born Americans, many immigrant families become more educated and financially secure over time. Their initial standard of living might be lower than that of native-born Americans, but compared to life in their countries of origin, they're generally better off. Their children experience more upward mobility than the average native-born American.

So what's to be done?

Proposals to reform immigration range from stricter limits and harsher penalties for illegal aliens to strategies to help them obtain legal work and citizenship. Before becoming president, U.S. Senator Barack Obama of Illinois, for instance, proposed that illegal immigrants pay a fine for breaking the law, but then earn the right to become permanent residents and eventually citizens. In addition, Obama, whose father came from Kenya, recommended a regulated flow of guest workers to replace the current flood of illegal immigrants. If such a program had been in place, Espinoza-Vazquez's parents might have been able to enter the country legally.

"It behooves us to remember that not every single immigrant who came into the United States through Ellis Island had proper documentation," said Obama. "But they came here in search of a dream, in search of hope. . . . Today's immigrants seek to follow in the same tradition of immigration that has built this country. We do ourselves and them a disservice if we do not recognize the contributions of these individuals."

her sister's son Johnny. The boy's crack-addled grandmother and unreliable mother left him in her care. Rushing and the two children lived in a $700-a-month apartment in Brooklyn.

Like many people in the missing class, Rushing's life rose and fell with the fortunes of her extended family. The reappearance of Yamika, Johnny's mother, in her son's life made things harder for Valerie. Yamika promised Johnny visits and gifts that never came. Bitterly disappointed, the boy started acting out in class. Rushing let Yamika move in with her on the condition that she contribute a modest $25 a week, and look after Johnny. However, before long, Yamika failed to live up to her end of the bargain. Finally, Rushing told her sister she'd have to leave in another two months.

Two years later, Newman and Chen found Rushing a changed woman. Her entire disposition seemed more cheerful. Yamika and Johnny had both moved out. Although Johnny was still misbehaving, his mother was finally ready to be a better parent. Valerie had moved to a larger apartment in Brooklyn. Looking back on the burden of taking care of Johnny, she said, "I did it because that was my nephew. I didn't want to see him in the system." But it took a toll on her. "Now that I can see what I can do on my own time by myself, I don't want to start over."

Rushing's story echoes those of many who struggle to make a better life for their children. Will Rushing's dreams of someday moving to the suburbs come true? Will she move up, stay the same, or backslide? Her future, and those of many others, undoubtedly will depend on the complex interactions between individual and societal responsibility.

3 Struggling Families

REBECCA WATCHED THE PINK "X" APPEAR ON THE dipstick.

She was pregnant. Another statistic. She froze in shock, her heart beating fast. Then she warmed to the idea of creating a new family with her boyfriend. But a few months later, they broke up. She gave birth and, with the help of supportive relatives and teachers, finished high school. She grew up alongside her baby.

Life proved to be harder than she expected. With bills to pay for the first time, Rebecca needed to go on welfare. Eventually, she landed a position as a paralegal trainee and got married, but she regrets that, as a teen, she acted more like a big sister than a mother to her daughter.

"Take it from someone who has been there," she wrote in her first-person story, originally published in the *St. Petersburg Times*. "It's up to each sexually active teenager to learn to protect himself or herself."

Antipoverty experts echo Rebecca's sentiments. Becoming a single parent, particularly as a teenager, increases one's chances of living in poverty because such families lack the financial cushion and resource pooling of two-wage-earner households. Many single mothers work long hours in low-wage jobs and are unable to afford quality child care. Thirty-two percent of families headed by a single parent are poor compared to only 7 percent of those headed by two married parents.

In America:

- One in three teenage girls gets pregnant each year.
- Half of first out-of-wedlock births are to teenagers.
- A child born to an unmarried teen mother who has not finished high school is nine times more likely to be poor than a child born to an adult parent who is married and has graduated from high school.

Teen Pregnancies and the "Abstinence Wars"

Cases like Rebecca's are typical. Although she did not plan to get pregnant, she didn't take action to prevent a pregnancy either. Often, such teens blame their pregnancies on "bad luck" or "being swept away" or say that it "just happened." Some girls see their pregnancy as a form of status. It's a ticket to adulthood in neighborhoods that offer few other opportunities.

Poverty is the single biggest determinant of teen pregnancy. While girls from poor and low-income families generally keep their babies, those from more advantaged backgrounds tend to choose abortion or, occasionally, adoption, because they see opportunities for themselves outside of motherhood. Girls in poor communities, on the other hand, often feel like they have nothing to lose by becoming mothers.

Because it's easier and more effective to prevent teen pregnancy than to deal with the negative social and economic consequences of such births, policy makers have made prevention a top priority. In the past decade, the teen pregnancy rate has dropped 36 percent. Researchers attribute much of the decline to better use of contraception and also speculate that new child-support provisions may be prompting young men to think twice before engaging in unprotected sex. The decline in teen pregnancy and, as a result, in the teen birthrate, is directly responsible for the 26 percent decrease in the number of children under age six living in poverty.

Young ballet dancers carry a cross into the ballroom of an annual Father/Daughter Purity Ball.

However, the so-called "abstinence wars" could stall future progress. Battle lines have formed over how best to teach sex education in public schools. In one camp are those who advocate teaching abstinence-only until marriage. In the other camp are advocates for comprehensive sexuality education, which includes contraception.

Research shows that students who take a "virginity pledge" as part of abstinence-only programs are just as likely to get pregnant or develop sexually transmitted diseases as nonpledgers. To break the deadlock over the abstinence wars, the Society for Adolescent Medicine has recommended a comprehensive approach that includes abstinence education as well as the correct and consistent use of condoms for teens who choose to be sexually active.

Many experts believe that sex education is not enough: Adolescents also need to see a brighter future. Programs such as Girls Inc. try to prevent teen pregnancy by giving students candid information about sexuality and providing after-school activities and mentors.

Seventeen-year-old Erika, for instance, dec ded to be different from her best friend, Maria, who got pregnant in high school. Although Maria tried to keep up with school through independent study, she found herself unable to balance schoolwork with the demands of parenting. Erika, on the other hand, began attending Girls Inc. and decided to go to college. "You can't sugar coat things like teen pregnancy and teen motherhood," she wrote.

Traditional Families Crumbling

In the 1950s, girls like Maria and Rebecca often married the fathers of their children. The stigma of out-of-wedlock births sent many teenage girls scurrying to the altar for "shotgun weddings." The 1960s heralded a cultural revolution that called for individual freedom. The old taboos against divorce and single parenting lost much of their sway. At around the same time, the loss of manufacturing jobs spelled economic uncertainty for many unskilled workers. Economic stress took a toll on couples, making some reluctant to get married and others more prone to divorce.

The old, two-parent family increasingly has given way to single-parent, cohabiting, and stepparent households. In 2000, one out of three children was born to unmarried parents. Single parents have become particularly common in black neighborhoods.

Concern about how single-parent families affect children has long provoked controversy. Are single parents somehow responsible for their own economic plight, or should society do more to help? In 1965, the question divided supporters from critics of a

Single mothers living in poverty often lack a social network or the education that might help them rise out of poverty. Drugs compound the problem. Katrena Hunt, addicted to crack, lives on the streets of Jackson, Mississippi, with her young daughter.

report written by then–assistant secretary of labor Daniel P. Moynihan, lamenting the rise of single motherhood in poor urban communities. Even though the report blamed the trend on rising male unemployment and called on the federal government to play a more active role in ensuring jobs for black men, critics of the Moynihan Report accused it of "blaming the victim."

However, since then, an extensive body of research has shown that family formations have decidedly public consequences. Children raised by two biological parents generally do better than those in other types of households. That's not to say, however, that children from single-parent families are doomed. Many do very well indeed. However, on average, children who grow up with only one biological parent (it's usually the mother) are more likely to develop behavioral problems, drop out of school, and end up in poverty than children from two-parent households.

Economic problems account for about half the negative outcomes, according to sociologist Sara McLanahan. Children in two-parent households (and, to a lesser extent, cohabiting families) benefit from pooled resources and because, if both work, there is more money coming in. But economics alone do not tell the full story. Because single parents do not have a partner with whom to share responsibilities, they cannot give their children as much time and attention as two parents. Low parental involvement, supervision, and aspirations, as well as greater residential mobility, contribute to the negative outcomes of children growing up with only one parent.

McLanahan uses the term "fragile families" to describe these households. Half of the relationships between single mothers and the fathers of their children end by the time the baby is five. Often, these women form new partnerships resulting in more children. While cohabitation and remarriage might increase income, they usually do not bring as many benefits as primary marriages.

Financial dealings in these fragile families often are shrouded in secrecy and rife with tension, researchers say. Should the new boyfriend pay for sneakers for a child from his girlfriend's prior relationship? Will a man jeopardize his relationship with his new wife if she knows he gives money to a child from a previous relationship? Married parents who are poor break up at twice the rate of non-poor families.

Many couples fearful of divorce put off marriage until they feel emotionally and financially secure. For some, that day never comes.

Human Capital and Social Capital

Experts see upward mobility in terms of both an individual's capabilities and his or her social supports. According to the *New*

Can Money Buy Happiness?

Researcher Dan Buettner has traveled the world to see where people are the happiest. Using results from elaborate questionnaires given to hundreds of thousands of men and women around the globe, Buettner points to Denmark as the happiest place on earth.

Denmark is hardly the tropical paradise one might associate with happiness. Still, people report high levels of contentment. The United States ranked twenty-third on the list, well behind Switzerland, Austria, Iceland, and the Bahamas, which placed second, third, fourth, and fifth respectively. Impoverished countries in Asia, on the other hand, have particularly low levels of happiness, with China 82nd, India 125th, and Russia 167th on the list.

The Danes pay some of the highest taxes in the world—between 50 percent and 70 percent of their incomes—but the government spends more money per capita on children and the elderly than any other country in the world. People describe themselves as feeling "tucked in," like a snug child.

"They have this thing called 'Jante-lov,' which essentially says, 'You're no better than anybody else,'" said Buettner, a best-selling author and world traveler. "A garbage man can live in a middle-class neighborhood and hold his head high."

Adrian White, an analytic social psychologist at the University of Leicester in England, has produced the first ever "world map of happiness." From analyzing a number of studies, he found a nation's level of happiness is most closely associated with health levels, followed by wealth, and then provision of education.

Studies show a strong correlation between poverty and unhappiness. Once people are able to get their basic needs met, they become much happier. But, beyond that, money doesn't make much difference, researchers say. While an American who earns $50,000 a year is apt to be twice as happy as someone who earns $20,000 a year, the payoff for surpassing $90,000 is slight. More money can lead to more stress. As the stocks plummet, so, too, do the moods of investors. Also, people tend to want more than they already have.

Numerous studies attest to the importance of health and social relationships on happiness. A survey by the University of Chicago's National Research Center, for example, found that respondents with five or more close friends were 50 percent more likely to describe themselves as "very happy" than those with smaller social circles.

Still, the role of money should not be overlooked. People who are struggling to get by often work long hours that take them away from those friends and relatives who can be such a tonic for happiness. "When you're richer, you can decide to work less—and spend more time with your friends," David Leonhardt wrote in the New York Times. "Affluence is a pretty good deal."

To combat homelessness and the disappearance of federal funds, charitable religious programs such as Habitat for Humanity sprang up in the 1980s. Here, teen volunteers help to build a home for a poor family.

York Times, sociologists use the terms "human capital" and "social capital" to describe the twin pillars of success:

- Human capital: a person's education, job credentials, and employability
- Social capital: emotional support from a reliable stakeholder in one's life, an asset commonly associated with marriage

Often, single mothers lack both kinds of capital. For three years, author Sharon Hays visited the homes of welfare offices and welfare clients to research her book *Flat Broke With Children: Women in the Age of Welfare Reform.* Hays found three patterns common among the welfare clients she interviewed:

- Domino effect of personal tragedy
- Inconsistent use of birth control
- Pushes toward work and pull toward home

Consider the case of "Sheila," a twenty-nine-year-old white woman identified by a pseudonym for reasons of confidentiality. Sheila's downward spiral began after her high school sweetheart was killed in an auto accident. Instead of going to college as planned, she took a part-time job and spent much of her time "sitting and mourning and moping and weeping." Then her father left her mother. Shortly afterward her mother developed blood clots in her legs, which made it impossible for her to work. Sheila lost her job, and she and her mother became homeless.

While homeless, Sheila met Sam, a man she saw as her savior because he let her and her mother move in with him. Sheila became pregnant before Sam, who was secretly married, left. Homeless again, Sheila was raped. She went on welfare, which allowed her to get a small studio to live in with her mother, who watched Sheila's daughter while Sheila took a string of temporary or low-paying jobs. Her luck seemed to turn for the better when she worked her way up to a management position in a fast-food restaurant. However, because the hours and the bus rides were so long, she quit that job. Whether she'd be able to find a more flexible position remained to be seen.

The Marriage Movement

Researchers who study people who have pulled themselves out of poverty into the ranks of the middle class point to the importance of work and marriage. But is marriage a realistic goal for the majority of single mothers?

Many experts say no. "Women who have children [from other relationships] are the least likely to find a mate," McLanahan said. Because of the high rates of joblessness and incarceration among black men, few poor single mothers find marriage a viable option. Only 1.4 percent of them marry in a given year, according to a 2002 study conducted by Signe-Mary McKernan and Caroline Ratcliffe of the Urban Institute. Of those who do, 56 percent are lifted out of poverty.

The PBS *Frontline* special, "Let's Get Married," profiled twenty-eight-year-old Ashaki, a single mother of seven on welfare. At the time, Ashaki was wrestling with the question of whether or not to marry her boyfriend, Steven, the father of her youngest child. *Frontline* met up with Ashaki at Family Focus, one of a growing number of programs that teach relationship skills to unmarried couples with children. Agencies typically approach unmarried couples at the "magic moment," the time around the birth of a child, when hopes and dreams soar. Relationship-skills classes typically address topics such as financial management and conflict resolution. In 2006, Congress allocated $750 million over five years for these programs to promote "healthy marriages" and "responsible fatherhood."

The Bush administration advocated the promotion of healthy marriages as a way to fight poverty and aid children. "You see, strong marriages and stable families are incredibly good for children," said then–president George W. Bush, in a speech, "and stable families should be the central goal of American welfare policy." President Obama has also pushed for strong, two-parent families. It is not yet clear how, or if, that will affect his administration's welfare policy.

However, critics of the marriage movement argue that couples need resources such as decent-paying jobs and child care before they can consider tying the knot. In some inner-city neighborhoods plagued by high rates of incarceration, unemployment, mental health problems, and violence, bridal shops are hard to find. A woman might have a child with a man but not regard him as marriage material.

Ashaki was a case in point. "I thought about marrying my oldest daughter's father," she told *Frontline*, "but we spent like ten years in and out of a relationship. He was kind of crazy. Violent, really."

Steven, on the other hand, won her over by helping with her children. He brought them to school and to the park. He even taught the five oldest children a dance routine to the Temptations song "My Girl." Ashaki lived in an apartment, which for weeks had no gas. She had to cook on a hot plate. Her relationship with Steven, though, blossomed. "You know, we just seem so right together," she said. "When I'm with him, it's, like, this is my soulmate. And I think that's why I want to marry him."

However Ashaki wanted certain things to be in place before getting married. She hoped for Steven to have a job. Steven, though, had trouble finding employment. To help Ashaki pay for milk and diapers, he sold drugs. Upon getting caught, he was sentenced to three months in boot camp. Ashaki put the marriage on hold. One of her daughters was so heartbroken, she drew a picture of the engagement ring Ashaki had pawned as a plea for the couple to stay together. Ashaki got the ring out of hock, but set no date for the wedding.

Whether relationship classes can help couples like Ashaki and Steven develop stable marriages remains to be seen. Many experts believe that such programs will have the best chance of success if they're linked to other supports, such as employment and mental-health services.

Researchers say that the future of children depends on a better system of supports for families. If a better system were in place, fathers could offer more financial support to their children. To do this, they would need jobs. In addition, sociologists like McLanahan call for better community resources such as after-school programs for all children. Many agree that it takes a village to raise a child.

4 Suburban Poverty

CHRISTOPHER GALE HATED GOING BACK TO SCHOOL after the winter break.

"Everyone else seemed to have everything, and we had nothing," he said. "My mom did her best. But it was awful going back to school after Christmas and seeing everyone's toys."

In suburbs like Christopher's, the "have-nots" brush up against the "haves" every day. The have-nots flip burgers and bag groceries to help their families while the haves buy expensive clothes and vacation in Paris. Some low-income suburbanites get the message they don't belong and have to hide their lack of money. Ada Estrella, for instance, pretended to live at a friend's house so her dates wouldn't have to drop her off at the trailer park. People in town called the Rolling Meadows trailer park "Rolling Ghettos."

While many people associate poverty with urban ghettos, poverty has sprawled into the suburbs. No longer are the suburbs the pristine retreat from urban ills shown in 1950s sitcoms. Since then, the suburbs have grown increasingly varied. Communities once known for their basketball hoops and manicured lawns have become sprinkled with boarded-up houses. Real-estate deals that seemed too good to be true proved to be just that. The downwardly mobile often point to some combination of a lost job, family breakup, and health problem that pushed them over the edge.

In recent years, the geographical locale of poverty has shifted. While in 1999 the majority of people below the poverty line lived in inner cities, by 2005 more of the nation's poor lived in the suburbs. Inner cities still hold the highest concentrations of poverty, but, overall, more people who are poor live in suburbs.

What accounts for this shift?

Researchers point to several trends. First, jobs increasingly have moved from central cities to the suburbs. Second, immigrants are moving directly to the suburbs, bypassing the major cities altogether. Third, gentrification of urban neighborhoods has forced some low-income residents to surrounding suburbs. The white flight of the past has given way to a new, reverse form of migration.

Being poor in the suburbs is a mixed bag. On the one hand, the suburbs offer some advantages over the inner cities. Because poverty is more hidden and dispersed in suburbs than in inner cities, the suburban poor are less likely to live in neighborhoods overcome by poverty-related crime and drug abuse.

But the suburbs also pose certain disadvantages. For one thing, cars are practically required, particularly in the outlying areas, because of spotty public transportation. Often people carpool to get to food pantries and soup kitchens that are scurrying to keep up with the rising demand for their services. At a soup kitchen in Hempstead, New York, for instance, manager Jean Victor used to make 20 pounds of pasta for lunch and have some left over. "Now we make 60 pounds, and there's none left over," she told a reporter.

Suburbs vary greatly from one another. While the rich suburbs are getting richer, the poor suburbs are getting poorer. A growing number of suburbs suffer from the same poor schools, crime, and drug abuse long linked to the inner city. Some observers call it the "urbanization of the suburbs."

"Throwaway" Mentality

Growing up in Chelsea, Massachusetts, Jay Ash got used to the smells. First, there was the stench of burnt rubber from the neighborhood rubber plant. Then came the exhaust fumes from the trucks. Finally, Ash remembers the stink of the oil tanks that always prompted his dad to yell, "Roll up your windows!"

Such memories belie the popular notion of the suburb as an idyllic place where birds chirp and flowers bloom. Once a summer resort for Boston's aristocracy, tiny Chelsea sprouted factories and triple-deckers for workers during the Industrial Revolution. Immigrants poured in, using Chelsea as a stepping-stone. It became what experts call a "first-tier suburb," an outgrowth of the nearby big city. Like residents of other first-tier suburbs, the immigrants of Chelsea worked hard so they could move their families to the more prosperous outlying towns. In the process, they left behind a decaying infrastructure and houses in need of repair.

"The deterioration we observed . . . serves as an indictment of the 'throwaway' mentality that seems to dominate our culture: build it, use it, exploit it, abandon it," author William Hudnut writes in his book, *Halfway to Everywhere: A Portrait of America's First-Tier Suburbs*. "In our consumer-oriented, disposal-minded society, houses, shops, neighborhoods, entire communities all go though an evolution that can end with a whimper."

For a while, Ash's family followed the traditional trajectory, moving from Chelsea to the leafier suburbs. The Ashes chose New Hampshire because of its low tax rate. But, in New Hampshire, his parents' marriage ended. At the age of eleven, Ash moved back to Chelsea with his mother and brother. They stayed with friends at first, then found a subsidized apartment in a triple-decker on a tiny lot of land.

"It was a close-knit neighborhood," said Ash, who is now in his forties. "You looked out for your neighbors, and, if you had problems, your neighbors were looking out for you as well."

Ash went away to college but returned to Chelsea in 1983 to become its city manager, an appointed position. The Poles, Jews, and Italians of his youth had given way to Latinos from Puerto Rico, Central America, and South America, as well as immigrants

Discount Stores Booming

Walk into any shopping mall, and you'll notice the difference.

The number of discount stores has mushroomed. Mid-level stores, on the other hand, are being squeezed out. Retailers such as Home Depot, Linens-n-Things, and Macy's have closed stores. The middle class isn't what it used to be.

Twenty years ago, middle-market department stores made up about 75 percent of the market while discounters like Wal-Mart and Kmart accounted for only 25 percent. Now it's the other way around. Discounters like Old Navy, Target, and H&M are turning out low-priced versions of the latest fashions.

Meanwhile, some mid-level stores like J.C. Penney and Kohl's have managed to stay afloat by cultivating a loyal customer base. To woo harried shoppers, a number of retailers tout online options. Some grocery stores are using more self-check registers to save on staffing costs as they face stiff competition from retailers such as Trader Joe's and Walgreens. Consumers appreciate bargains in this era of stagnant wages.

Still, experts say, even financially strapped consumers want to splurge from time to time. "People will find the one thing they really love and blow their doors out for that and make up for it by cutting back elsewhere," consultant Jon Berry told *Retail Traffic*. "They will budget in one area to get a treat in another."

from Asia and Africa. Factories closed down. While young people in Ash's day engaged in fistfights and car thefts, the new generation lived in a world of drugs, guns, knives, and gangs. The city plunged into a financial crisis leading to state receivership in 1991.

After Chelsea regained its financial autonomy in 1995, new plans called for sweeping improvements. Chelsea's schools developed a partnership with Boston University. The city began acquiring old factories with the plan of turning them into housing. New galleries opened up. Young professionals attracted by Chelsea's proximity to Boston bought lofts in buildings that once manufactured cardboard boxes.

Still, poverty remains. In this ethnically diverse community, approximately half the residents identify themselves as Hispanic/Latino, about one third Caucasian, 12 percent Southeast Asian, 2 percent African American, and 2 percent African/Afro-Caribbean. As Ash sees it, Chelsea caters to first-generation immigrants who are bound to be poor. Some new immigrants rise up the economic ladder, but not everyone makes that leap.

"Today it's more difficult to make that step up," Ash says. "Italian bricklayers lived in a simpler time."

Tensions over Immigration

In the primarily middle-class suburb of Farmingville, New York, two Mexican day laborers waited outside a convenience store one morning for their work assignments. Two white men pulled up, pretending to be contractors. Instead, they brought the two immigrants to an abandoned industrial park and attacked them with a pole-hole digger and a knife. The Mexican laborers barely escaped with their lives. The two attackers were convicted of attempted manslaughter and sentenced to twenty-five years in prison.

This attack in a small Long Island town illustrates the growing resentments of native-born Americans to the influx of immigrants in America's suburbs. Poverty exists not only in the first-tier suburbs but also in the surrounding towns, where new jobs have sprouted up in restaurants, strip malls, construction sites, and in the homes of well-heeled residents looking for gardeners and nannies. In these towns, affordable housing remains in short supply.

In Farmingville, a town of bungalows and ranch houses broken up by strip malls, day laborers and their families have crowded into the tiny single-family homes. Resentment of immigrants has grown among suburbanites who worry that their property values are being jeopardized by overcrowding, increased traffic, and strained municipal services. Some townspeople have called day laborers "parasites" and thrown rocks at them.

How authorities respond to complaints varies from suburb to suburb. In Farmingville, for instance, the police locked up eleven houses said to be dangerously overcrowded and evicted about two hundred tenants. The tenants, who were living in packed conditions some observers compared to the turn-of-the-century tenements, set up a tent city behind one of the houses in protest. In North Hempstead, New York, on the other hand, Nassau County officials helped tenants in overcrowded buildings find alternative housing. Tom Suozzi, the executive for Nassau County on Long Island, told *USA Today* that officials needed to find a delicate balance.

"Long-term residents have a legitimate concern that illegal housing is dangerous and devalues their neighborhoods," said Suozzi, the son of an Italian immigrant. "But day laborers and immigrant activists have a legitimate concern, also, that this issue cannot be used as an excuse for racism. So finding that balance is one of the tough challenges that exist."

While political leaders ponder plans for immigration reform, conflicts over immigration have pitted neighbor against neighbor, community against community. Some towns have passed exclusionary zoning to keep the people they employ in their homes, stores, and restaurants from moving in. In response, advocacy groups and community leaders who support immigrant rights

Hispanic day laborers crowd around a sport-utility vehicle in this suburban Long Island community, hoping to get temporary work.

have adopted a new rallying cry: "If you're good enough to work here, you're good enough to live here."

Many observers attribute the resentment of immigrants to the middle-class's growing sense of "being squeezed" by the tight economy. Stressed-out suburbanites are looking for someone to blame. Experts, though, see a lack of economic opportunity as the real culprit.

"A strong middle class is the best ally of the poor," writes Elizabeth Warren, a professor at Harvard Law School. "A middle class that is rich with opportunity opens the paths out of poverty. A middle class that is financially strong can support the programs needed to give the poor a helping hand. A middle class that is prosperous provides the model for how education and hard work pay off."

Middle-Class Anxieties

Karen Volkman's neighborhood in Minnesota reflects the problems of a vanishing middle class. Since Volkman, a forty-three-year-old postal worker, bought her modest home in 1993, her neighborhood has changed completely. Several houses lie vacant, and empty lots stand where a bowling alley and jewelry store used to be.

"I'm not as happy with the neighborhood as when I bought it," Volkman told the *St. Paul Pioneer Press*. "People just don't take care of their stuff as much."

Boarded-up houses are signs of the foreclosure crisis besieging the nation. Since the 1970s, the number of Americans unable to pay their mortgages has increased fivefold. In 2008, Lawrence Summers, now the head of the National Economic Council in the Obama administration, predicted an additional 2 million foreclosures over the next two years. Home ownership has increasingly become a challenge for the middle-class and working-class residents who make up America's mainstream.

Maryanne Hernandez, for instance, bought her dream house in San Bernardino, California, in 2003. By 2007, she had fallen four months behind in her mortgage payments. "It's not just us," Hernandez told Reuters news service. "It's all over."

Analysts blame much of the mortgage problem on the "sub-prime lending crisis." The term "sub-prime" refers to borrowers with low credit ratings from not paying their bills on time. Lenders have lured prospective home owners with poor credit by offering them attractive deals. The catch is that payments increase over time. Many borrowers gambled on themselves, thinking they could meet the payments, and lost.

A Dog and His Owner

The foreclosure crisis has trickled down to tenants. In Milwaukee County, Kevin Pittman, a thirty-seven-year-old self-employed carpenter and lawn-equipment repairman, returned home from

Car Repossessions Speed Up

Life has been very good lately for the "repo man."

That's the nickname of the person charged with repossessing cars. In recent years, repo rates have doubled, according to an industry source. Like the increase in home foreclosures, the rise in defaults on car loans can be linked to attractive deals that snag consumers in a web of rising interest rates. Owners can't keep up with their payments, so they end up on the radar screen of the repo man.

Stories of fights, confrontations, and shoot-outs with angry car owners who don't want to surrender their keys have dogged the repossession industry. Kevin J. McGivern, president of Equitable Services Inc., a repo firm in Illinois, told a reporter he hasn't experienced any violent confrontations.

"It's not a blood and guts business," he explained. "We do a lot of our repo business by talking to people first."

Sometimes the sight of the repo man is a relief. An owner tired of sinking money into skyrocketing gas rates and steep monthly payments might gladly turn over the car keys.

But, often, a car repossession sets in motion a downward spiral. The person who bought the car is left with no way to get to work and poor credit. Some people work out an extension on their loan, but, even so, the continued payments might be a bitter pill to swallow. Many owners regret being talked into their deals by aggressive car salespeople.

"We got swindled and overpriced," Carole Beausoleil, fifty-eight, of Southbridge, Massachusetts, told the *Boston Globe*. "It was a mistake, and now it's too late."

work one day to find his dog, Patches, scrabbling frantically in a cage. Pittman's breakfast dishes sat in the sink. The bank had foreclosed on the house that he rented, so the sheriff came to haul away Pittman's belongings.

Pittman, who was shocked because he thought he had more time to vacate the premises, rescued Patches from a possible trip to the pound. The sheriff's deputies told him they were sorry; they knew the foreclosure wasn't his fault. Pittman told them his wife had recently died, leaving him to care for their six children.

"We don't have anyplace to go," Pittman told the *Milwaukee Journal Sentinel.* "Who's going to rent to a man with six kids and a dog?"

The sheriff arranged with the creditor's attorney to let Pittman stay three more days. Meanwhile, across the nation, other suburbanites faced similarly uncertain futures. Many employers have slashed benefits, closed factories, or sent jobs overseas.

David Lamberger, for example, used to work as an auto-parts maker in Detroit, Michigan. After he lost his job, he found work at a used-car lot that pays a much less certain salary. Lamberger and his family risk losing their home to foreclosure.

"There have been years I made $80,000, and there have been years I made $28,000," Lamberger told the *Detroit Free Press.* "Sometimes we're able to pay bills and get by, but then stuff from the slow times never goes away. You can't catch up, and it comes back to haunt you."

Families like the Lambergers are hard-pressed to save money because their fixed expenses are so high. While the typical one-income family was putting away around 11 percent of its take-home pay in savings in the 1970s, the typical household a generation later had picked up a second paycheck but spent more money than it saved.

iPods and DVDs

Where did all the money go? Have Americans frittered away all their disposable income on iPods, DVDs, and other consumer goods?

Not really, experts say. Although Americans are spending about 23 percent more on electronics, they're paying less for other consumer goods. Americans are buying fewer dressy clothes and doing more shopping at discount stores, according to Harvard law school professor Elizabeth Warren.

What's gone up—way up—are fixed expenses. Families in the twenty-first century pay considerably more for housing, health care, transportation, and child care than their counterparts a generation ago. Warren points to the following changes since the early 1970s:

- The home mortgage has ballooned from $465 to $854 a month.
- Families spend 74 percent more on health insurance.
- Overall transportation costs for a family of four have increased by 52 percent.
- Today's family with one preschooler and one child in elementary school lays out an average of $1,048 a month for care for the children compared to no child-care costs when someone was home full time.

Often, to pay these bills, people trim food expenses and work extra jobs. In the 1970s, when a child was ill or grandma broke her hip, a family member could provide the care. Today, on the other hand, everyone is working. Many of the stressed-out, financially insecure middle-class families of the twenty-first century live paycheck to paycheck, sharing an uncertain future with the nation's poor. Warren believes that poverty is a problem that demands wide-ranging solutions.

"The solutions to poverty do not lie with problems aimed only toward the poor," she writes in her essay, "The Vanishing Middle Class." "The solutions lie with reuniting America, led by a strong middle class that looks forward to an even brighter future."

5 Urban Poverty

IS AMERICA A LAND OF OPPORTUNITY OR A NATION that keeps African Americans trapped in a cycle of urban poverty?

The complex answer to this question got a new twist in 2008 when Barack Obama made history by becoming the nation's first African-American president. Many African Americans—and, in fact, Americans of all colors and ethnicities—wept with joy because they never thought they'd see the day when a black person reached the country's highest office. The election showed that change had come to America. Economic issues trumped race. In a *Time* magazine poll, voters overwhelmingly—by a ratio of more than nine to one—responded that race would not be an issue in how they voted.

Still, the rise of an exceptional individual like Obama, the son of a white woman from Kansas and a black man from Kenya, does not negate the problems of urban poverty or the existence of negative racial stereotypes. An Associated Press poll, for instance, found that one third of white respondents agreed with at least one negative generalization of blacks. The stereotypes include that blacks are "lazy," "violent," or responsible for their own troubles.

What can be done to dispel such stereotypes?

Many African-American leaders—President Obama included —believe that, while the nation needs to fight prejudice, blacks also need to take responsibility for their own behavior. In a speech before the National Association for the Advancement of Colored People

President Barack Obama, himself raised primarily by his mother after she and his father divorced, has called for African-American parents to take more responsibility for the upbringing of their children.

(NAACP), Obama said, "Now, I know there's some who've been saying I've been too tough talking about responsibility. But here at the NAACP, I'm here to report I'm not going to stop talking about it. Because—no matter how many ten-point plans we propose, or how many government programs we launch—none of it will make any difference if we don't seize more responsibility in our lives."

The African-American community has long been divided over how much emphasis to place on personal responsibility and how much on societal factors. Legendary entertainer Bill Cosby, for instance, emphasizes the former. As the famous entertainer sees it, an array of negative behaviors has trapped African Americans in the ghetto. High dropout rates. Teen pregnancy. Children abandoned by their fathers. Drugs. Crime. Gangsta rap. And a poor command of standard English.

"You can't land a plane in Rome saying 'Whassup?' to the control tower," he writes with coauthor Alvin F. Poussaint, M.D., in his latest book *Come on People: On the Path from Victims to Victors.* "You can't be a doctor telling your nurse, 'Dat tumor be nasty.'"

Cosby has long emphasized the importance of education. Some pundits credit *The Cosby Show* with presenting an appealing middle-class black family, the Huxtables, to lay the groundwork for Obama's victory. Cosby, though, suggests looking beyond the influence of the TV family to that of the real family in which Obama was raised. Cosby cites the president's account of being woken early to do his homework and his mother's refusal to accept any excuses.

Like Cosby, President Obama urges African-American fathers to take responsibility for their children. He, himself, was raised by a single mother after his father left home. In addition to sounding the theme of family responsibility, Obama's address to the NAACP linked civil rights to economic rights:

"[I]t doesn't matter if you have the right to sit at the front of the bus if you can't afford the bus fare," he said. "It doesn't matter if you have the right to sit at the lunch counter if you can't afford the lunch."

While welfare reform has brought some gains to black women and other groups, researchers say that poor black men are being left behind. New studies by experts at Columbia, Princeton, and Harvard universities, and at other institutions show rising black male drop-out rates, joblessness, and incarceration. Here are some of the findings:

- In the inner cities, more than half of all blacks do not finish high school.

- 72 percent of black male high school dropouts in their twenties were jobless, compared to 34 percent of white and 19 percent of Hispanic dropouts.
- By their mid-thirties, six in ten black men who had dropped out of school had spent time in prison.
- About half of all black men in their twenties and early thirties who did not go to college are noncustodial fathers.
- More black dropouts are in prison on a given day—34 percent—than are working.

Experts say that factors such as a sluggish economy, the loss of manufacturing jobs, inadequately funded inner-city schools, and poor child care affect behavior. In the inner city, drug-related arrests are common. Although African Americans make up only 13 percent of drug users, they comprise 38 percent of those arrested for drug offenses and 59 percent of those convicted of drug offenses, according to the Drug Policy Alliance Network. Blacks also are overrepresented among homicide victims and convictions. The U.S. Bureau of Justice Statistics reported that, in 2005, black homicide victimization rates were six times higher and offending rates seven times higher than the rates for whites.

Crime and despair have long plagued inner-city neighborhoods. Cosby himself grew up poor in an inner-city neighborhood in Philadelphia. The legendary entertainer, who holds a doctorate in education, recently returned to his alma mater, the University of Massachusetts at Amherst, to deliver his message of self-help. Wearing a UMass sweatshirt, he sounded an urgent plea:

"I'm trying to stop the bloodshed," he told a packed auditorium. During the question-and-answer period, a few members of the audience criticized his message.

A Difficult Journey

Carlos McBride, a thirty-eight-year-old graduate student and youth mentor, approached the microphone. Having grown up in an urban neighborhood in Springfield, Massachusetts, he took issue with Bill Cosby's self-help approach.

"You can't put your finger in someone's face and say, 'Do good in school,'" McBride maintained. "There is nothing anyone could have told me that would have made me want to do this. I'm tired of feeling like it's an easy solution."

McBride's life story shows how the threads of personal and societal responsibility are often woven together. The son of a father who abused drugs and a mother who drank too much, Carlos dropped out of school after ninth grade and spent his days hanging out with his African-American and Puerto Rican friends. He fathered two children out of wedlock and got his nickname "REC" for being reckless. He took pride in his daring. Sometimes he ran drugs from New York City to western Massachusetts.

In some ways, though, McBride's family defied the stereotype of the dysfunctional poor. His mother always cooked, and his father read books of philosophy. After his parents separated when he was about nine years old, his father carried off eight garbage bags full of books. His grandmother looked after her big family, asking Carlos, who already had two children of his own, to take in his little cousin. "I know you're going to do something great," she told him.

Her faith in him planted a seed, but McBride wasn't yet ready to leave the streets. Even though he worked in a factory from seven at night until seven in the morning, he also felt the tug of the illegal economy. He told his father about his plans to carry out a small robbery. "I just want to tell you how much I love you," the elder McBride said. "Think about what you're doing."

His father's words began to take hold as the gun violence escalated. The elder McBride had recently gotten out of drug rehab and was doing well. Carlos, on the other hand, had lost one friend after another to death or prison. Once he watched as a friend was gunned down outside a nightclub. Finally, in his early twenties, a conflict with his landlady sent him to court. After he

Being born into poverty isn't necessarily a life sentence. Virginia Tech graduate Carolyn Barnes, once homeless, is heading to the University of Michigan to pursue a doctorate in political science and public policy. The way out of poverty is paved with education and help from mentors and public funding.

got probation, McBride decided to turn his life around. He entered an innovative program, the Learning Tree, which helped him make the transition to a special scholarship program at prestigious Hampshire College.

It wasn't easy, though. McBride felt like an outsider at first. He held onto his gun for a while, brandishing it after some kids ridiculed him for being Puerto Rican, calling out, "Hey Julio Iglesias." The kids offered him money. He put away the gun and eventually gave it to a friend.

Then one of his professors helped him believe in himself. She told him, "I honestly believe you're an amazing writer." He got his poem, "Ghetto Thang," published in an anthology.

These days, McBride juggles his Ph.D. program in literacy education at the University of Massachusetts with teaching at local community colleges, hosting a hip-hop radio show, and mentoring young people. On one arm, a graffiti-style tattoo spells out "Reckless." On his other arm, a large tattoo proclaims "Knowledge is Power."

Urban Poem

mental breakdown
© by carlos rec mcbride

    my heart was beating out of place . . .
   all of a sudden i heard a click
  BOOM!!!

 that was it . . . i was hit.
i fell down to my knees 2 stunned 2 plead
i began to feel the blood trickle down my sleeves,
the kids ran realizing . . . i wasn't their man.

DAMN!!!
i'm being taken out of this game
who's to blame?
will our race ever reign?
i mean will the warfare ever disappear
where brothas and sistas can roam in any zone
being able to come and go
without getting filled with bullet holes?
with all this artillery, we could start our own army,
then they would see
the men who run this country . . .
the real vandals
pullin' off enron scandals
telling us how to live
enforcing curfews on our kids
provide more jobs so we wouldn't have to rob . . .
building more prisons are their visions of helping us out . . .

This is an excerpt from Carlos REC McBride's poem, "Mental Breakdown."
McBride teaches a course in hip-hop culture at Greenfield Community College
in Greenfield, Massachusetts.

His rise from the streets to academia didn't happen overnight. He needed to see for himself that the risks of crime outweighed the benefits and, in the process, find people who believed in him and programs able to give him a helping hand. These days, he keeps one foot in academia and the other in the urban terrain.

"Instead of a harsh approach like a slap on the hand, I try to relate to where kids are at," he says about his mentoring work. "I'm just as real as possible. How do you tell kids to just focus when they're not getting what they need?"

Poverty Is "Contagious"

The housing development where Rachel lived was being torn down. Rachel (who was identified by her first name only) had a choice: She could either move to another housing project or use Section 8 vouchers to find an apartment on the private market.

Like most of the other people in her housing development, she chose the Section 8 option. She wanted a better environment for her four children. Even though her old housing development felt like home, only about a third of the adults were employed. Rachel, who worked full time, moved to a more integrated neighborhood with less joblessness. She found the neighborhood a step up because everyone worked, and no one had time for "nonsense."

Experiences like Rachel's stem from new policies such as the U.S. Department of Housing and Urban Development's HOPE VI program, which aims to relocate the poor from blighted, high-density, overwhelmingly minority urban projects to other options. Even though racial segregation persists, researchers have seen a decline in the number of inner-city neighborhoods in which more than 40 percent of residents, the so-called "underclass," live below the poverty line. Participants in programs such as HOPE VI describe their new neighborhoods as less problematic but also less friendly than their old ones.

Social ties take years to build, experts say. "An effort needs to be made to connect relocated families with institutions in their new neighborhoods and to foster strong cross-status ties in mixed-income neighborhoods—either in newly redeveloped HOPE VI sites or in their new neighborhoods," writes Susan Clampet-Lundquist, a postdoctoral fellow at the Center for Research on Child Wellbeing at Princeton University.

Neighborhoods with high concentrations of poverty remain. Political economist Paul Jargowsky calls them places where "the poor . . . not only have to cope with their own poverty but also that of those around them." Studies show that the majority of people convicted of crimes live in just such heavily concentrated neighborhoods. According to the Justice Mapping Center, a Brooklyn-based research group, more than 50 percent of adult male inmates from New York City come from just fourteen districts in Manhattan, the Bronx, and Brooklyn. Eric Cadora of the Justice Mapping Center calls them "million dollar blocks" because that's what it costs the state to keep criminals from those areas behind bars. Instead of rehabilitating prisoners, some policy experts recommend rehabilitating the neighborhoods that produce them.

Harvard University professor William Julius Wilson and other experts see a strong link between joblessness and criminal behavior. As Wilson sees it, many problems of America's inner-city ghetto neighborhoods—crime, family dissolution, welfare, low levels of social organization, and so on—are related to the disappearance of work in the formal labor market. While many of the officially jobless participate in informal or illegal kinds of work such as baby-sitting or drug dealing, such activities place less of a premium on the daily behaviors of discipline, regularity, and stability that govern the formal workplace. Neighborhoods of high joblessness lack the kind of mainstream vitality that discourages illicit activities such as drug trafficking, crime, prostitution, and the formation of gangs.

One resident of a high-joblessness neighborhood on the South Side of Chicago lamented the lack of services for children. He told

At one time, public housing projects such as this one in south Chicago helped people get a leg up out of even more dire poverty; too often, in modern-day America, they become traps.

Wilson: "There's no library for them [children] to go to. There's not a centre they can go to, there's no field house that they can go into. There's nothing. There's nothing at all."

The gap between educated middle-class blacks and the ghetto poor has widened in recent years. Policy makers are well aware that the attempt to boost jobs and education in the inner-city may be a daunting task. In some schools, African-American achievers have been taunted for "acting white."

Schools of Hard Knocks

Cedric Jennings hid in the chemistry room in his inner-city high school during the awards ceremony. A top student, he couldn't face the abuse classmates heaped on those awarded one-hundred-dollar checks for making the honor roll.

"Nerd!"

"Geek!"

"Egghead."

And, worst of all, "Whitey!"

Such insults, chronicled in Pulitzer Prize–winning journalist Ron Suskind's book, *A Hope in the Unseen: An American Odyssey from the Inner City to the Ivy League*, illustrate a longstanding myth in the African-American community that being bookish means you're "acting white." Educators call it the "crab in the bucket syndrome." When one crab tries to climb out of the bucket, the other crabs pull it back down.

Many observers believe that President Obama's victory provides new encouragement for African Americans to achieve. In an article in *New York* magazine titled "Revenge of the Black Nerd," John McWhorter writes, "Whenever a black nerd gets teased for thinking he's white, all he has to say is four words: 'Is Barack Obama white?'"

Cedric Jennings's journey from a poor urban school to Brown University shows that students in even the most troubled schools can succeed. But to do so requires the kind of heroism not expected of students from more privileged schools. Nationwide, researchers say, the difference in per-pupil spending between districts with the highest numbers of minorities and those with the fewest amounts to more than $25,000 for a typical class in elementary school.

Author Jonathan Kozol criticizes the trend as a return to the old days of "separate but equal." Minority students in the inner cities, he says, feel the sting of racial isolation. A fifteen-year-old girl in Harlem told him, "It's like we're being hidden."

The inequalities begin early in life. Studies show that the children of impoverished families enter school with lower language skills and prereading skills than children from professional families.

Take the case of two-year-old Safiya. Profiled, along with her mother Danielle Wayne, in Katherine Newman and Victor Tan

Chen's book *The Missing Class: Portraits of the Near Poor in America,* Safiya possessed an extraordinarily limited vocabulary. Her one stock phrase: "SHUDDUP!"

Wayne, who worked full time, had less time for Safiya than she had for her two elder daughters when she was on welfare. Unable to afford to enroll Safiya in a child-care center, Wayne instead left her with her mother-in-law. There, the *Jerry Springer Show* played on the TV, and two young men smoked marijuana in the back room.

Safiya's future hangs in the balance as educators wrestle with a number of thorny issues. How can they attract successful teachers to inner-city schools? What kind of tests or other measurements should be used to gauge success? And, perhaps most important, how can teachers and staff build strong relationships with students?

After Cedric Jennings graduated from Brown University, he worked a variety of jobs and got a master's degree in social work. In the course of his journey, he met Supreme Court Justice Clarence Thomas. The conservative African-American justice warned Cedric that he could end up "caught between two worlds." Cedric returned to his hometown of Washington, D.C., where he has worked as a social worker and youth minister. He co-organized a college night at his church that was well attended. The event has given him a new sense of hope that he might be able to live in one world, not two, bridging the racial divide.

Just what Obama's presidency will mean for the nuts and bolts of education policy remains to be seen. However, his victory undoubtedly shows the rewards of hard work and education. On the eve of the 2008 election, Angela Cox, a forty-three-year-old Florida high school teacher, wept as Obama took the stage. "For the first time, I see my students really believe that skin color really doesn't matter," she said, shaking.

6 Rural Poverty

DR. EDWIN SMITH SEES POVERTY IN THE MOUTHS OF his patients.

Driving his mobile dental clinic through the hills of Appalachia, he meets people who have used Krazy Glue to reattach broken teeth. He treats patients who have pulled out their own infected teeth with pliers because they couldn't afford a dentist. And he sees the rotted and blackened teeth that are a side effect of methamphetamine drug use.

"The level of need is hard to believe unless you see it up close," Smith told the *New York Times*. Most of the people he encounters are too busy putting food on the table to worry about oral hygiene. Adults with teeth lost to sweets, tobacco, and/or neglect often have trouble finding work. Children frequently miss school because of pain caused by dental problems.

Such signs of poverty abound in rural America, where people often have to drive for miles to find goods and services. In a nation known for its scenic vistas of mountains and prairies, many rural residents live in grinding poverty, suffering from inadequate health care, a deficit of federal support, dwindling economic opportunities, and isolation from the rest of the nation. Settlements with fewer than 2,500 residents are considered rural. Statistics paint a bleak picture of the economic health of rural America:

- 340 of the nation's 386 "persistently poor" counties—
  those with 20 percent or more of the population living
  in poverty—are rural.

Poverty is just as daunting in rural areas as it is in urban areas. The Call family lives in a trailer in rural Maine. They subsist on the husband's disability checks, food stamps, and fuel assistance.

- Rural communities occupy 80 percent of the nation's land but make up only 20 percent of its population.
- Six of every ten rural areas lag behind the national economy in terms of adding new jobs.

Because of its distance from major metropolitan markets, rural America rarely gets covered in the media unless there's some major tragedy. As a result, country folk are often stereotyped, ignored, or simply forgotten.

"Rural people are either characters out of *Deliverance* or *Mayberry R.F.D.*—outright depravity and social disintegration on one hand or overly romanticized folksiness and neo-Jeffersonian virtue on the other," writes Mark B. Lapping in *Planning* magazine.

He adds, "Another stereotype is that most rural Americans are farmers. In fact, with less than two percent of the entire U.S. population engaged in agriculture, farming occupies an ever smaller niche in our rural economy."

In rural America, job seekers often find little more than a McDonald's and a supermarket for miles on end. Wages in rural areas lag behind those in urban America. The old days of the self-sufficient family farm have long passed. These days, someone in a sparsely populated part of the country might need to drive 25 miles to the nearest supermarket. For many rural Americans, a car is both a blessing and a curse. On the one hand, it opens up job opportunities. On the other hand, it sucks up money for gas and repairs.

Rural America resembles a patchwork quilt in its diversity of regions and people. Some rural areas have found a way to cash in on their scenic beauty by developing recreation and retirement, the so-called R&R industry. Others, though, lack such basic amenities as roads and telecommunications to attract newcomers.

Some regions have been particularly hard hit by poverty. The Pacific Northwest, for instance, has been dubbed the "new Appalachia" because of its loss of logging jobs. The so-called Black Belt of the Mississippi Delta lays claim to the enduring poverty of rural African Americans. In a growing swatch of the country, migrant workers harvest crops and work menial jobs in meat-packing and food-processing plants. And on the Indian reservations of rural America, indigenous people wrestle with the highest poverty rates in the nation.

American Indians

At the Pine Ridge (Sioux) Reservation in South Dakota, poverty lies hidden away in a desert of grass. There are no banks, discount stores, libraries, or movie theaters. The U.S. Census Bureau has proclaimed Pine Ridge the poorest county in the nation, with 75 percent of the population unemployed. According to writer Stephanie M. Schwartz, the reservation's residents "live in abject, incomprehensible conditions rivaling, or even surpassing, that of many Third World countries."

More specifically:

- about 97 percent of the population lives below federal poverty levels;
- alcoholism affects eight out of ten families on the reservation;
- the teenage suicide rate is 150 percent higher than the U.S. national average for this age group;
- the school drop-out rate is over 70 percent;
- 33 percent of the reservation homes lack basic water and sewage systems as well as electricity.

The Sioux are not alone in their plight. In Indian country, 26 percent of the population lives below the poverty line, twice the national average. American Indians have the highest teen suicide rate of any ethnic group in the nation.

Nevertheless, tribal leaders have not given up hope. The Sioux at Pine Ridge have developed innovative proposals for new culture and language programs, business development, substance abuse treatment, and alternative education initiatives. However, funding for such programs remains uncertain.

While the Sioux oppose gambling on religious grounds, other tribes have established casinos to lift their people out of poverty. The results have been mixed. Some casinos have brought not only great wealth but also a new set of problems for the tribe.

Consider the case of Foxwoods Casino in the southeastern corner of Connecticut. Established on the site of an old Pequot tribe reservation, the casino brought the Pequot back from the brink of extinction. In the early 1970s, only Elizabeth George and her sister remained in a dilapidated house on the Pequot reservation, which lacked electricity, roads, and businesses. When the state threatened to turn the ancestral land into a park, the elderly George pleaded with her relatives to return to the reservation.

Soon after George died in 1973, her grandson, Richard "Skip" Hayward, moved onto the site. Hayward, a pipe fitter and welder,

The Navajo Nation has rejected the casino gambling that has brought riches to many American Indian tribe because they equate its excesses with alcoholism. Instead, many tribe members live in poverty.

wrote to faraway relatives, urging them to join him, and some did. It was touch-and-go at first, but the group's luck changed for the better once they opened a high-stakes bingo parlor in 1986. Two years later, the federal government passed the Indian Gaming Regulatory Act, allowing the tribe to expand its bingo hall into a casino.

Requests poured in from people claiming to be Pequot. If individuals could trace their family lineage back to a Pequot listed in a 1900 or 1910 census, they could claim membership in the tribe. Membership and revenue swelled. Limos snaked through the town. Within five years of its opening, the glitzy attraction grossed over $1 billion annually. Mansions and luxury cars dotted the new gated community. Under the tribe's profit-sharing plan, each member, eighteen and over, working or not, would receive about $100,000 a year.

But, with unprecedented wealth and power came a new set of problems. Many young people felt no need to work or go to school. Some took drugs. Internal dissension rocked the tribe. Racial tensions flared. Dissatisfaction with Hayward's leadership grew. In 1998, he lost his bid to retain the chairmanship.

Of the 560 federally recognized tribes, only 200 have established casinos. Of these, fewer than twenty have generated substantial wealth for their members. Many casinos are located in areas too remote to be profitable.

Migrant Workers

Norma Flores stood under the scorching sun, drenched in sweat, with an acre or more of weeds to hoe. It was a typical July day for Flores, a teenager who worked alongside her parents in the fields twelve hours a day, seven days a week, every summer. She had the sunburn, aches, and rashes to show for her hard work.

"As you stand in the middle of the field and look around you, your mind is swarmed with millions of reasons why to pursue a college education," Flores, eighteen, wrote in an essay for Motivation Education & Training, Inc., a nonprofit organization that serves farmworkers. "Being a migrant also served as an opportunity to see what a sacrifice my parents have gone through to give us the opportunity to achieve all our dreams."

Migrant workers like Flores make up a group of Americans some experts call "the poorest of the poor." Children who work on farms are governed by different laws than those in any other occupation. While the minimum employment age for nonagricultural work is fourteen, young farm laborers can start at age twelve if accompanied by a parent. Youth who are fourteen or older can work unlimited hours in the fields before or after school hours. Those in other occupations are permitted to work only three hours per day while school is in session.

Many young people in migrant families start the school year late and end early so they can work the spring, summer, and fall crops. To stay at grade level, they often cram in extra homework before they leave or mail it in to their hometown schools. Nevertheless, participants in programs for migrant workers also describe a positive side to the work. Families working in the fields develop a special kind of closeness during their long days together.

Farmworkers toil in blistering heat and drenching rains. Many suffer injuries and poor health from exposure to pesticides. Painful welts and sore bodies from heavy picking bags are common. Some unscrupulous bosses berate workers and push them to work harder and faster than reasonably possible. If laborers complain about their conditions or try to organize, employers might threaten to fire or deport them.

The workers have reason to be afraid. During the administration of President George W. Bush, the Department of Labor tilted toward employers and failed to enforce labor laws. In particular, the Bush administration's order of increased checks of Social Security numbers has created a wave of fear among illegal immigrants who have invented a string of digits or borrowed identification that belongs to someone else. Immigrants who protest working conditions run the risk of being fired. An article in the *Nation* describes how employers benefit from the Bush administration's immigration policies: "Increased fear and vulnerability makes immigrant labor cheaper, by making it riskier to protest bad conditions, or ask for higher wages."

Past Mistakes and Future Hopes

By her own admission, Gwen Boggs had "messed up." At the age of fifteen, she began running with a bad crowd in her small mining town in Appalachia. She stayed up all hours, drinking and smoking marijuana, dropped out of high school, and got pregnant. After marrying and working in a variety of fast-food restaurants, Gwen decided she wanted a better life for her children.

"A Little Meth and a Lot of Booze"

In the American West, big skies, green pastures, and majestic mountains stretch on for miles. Yet, against this seemingly idyllic backdrop, an unusually high percentage of young people are drinking to excess, vomiting, passing out, and sometimes dying in alcohol-related car crashes.

Why so much heavy drinking in rural America? Insiders point to one main reason: boredom. With little to do outside of organized sports, many young people cluster in barns and mountain hideaways to get intoxicated. Townspeople in old frontier towns commonly regard drinking as a rite of passage.

"We're a frontier culture, and people say, 'I work hard and I'll be damned if I'm not going to have a beer or two on the way home,'" Rosie Buzzas, a Montana legislator, told the *New York Times*. "There's a church, a school, and 10 bars in every town."

Drugs, too, have made their way into small towns long associated with such wholesome activities as 4H Clubs and church bazaars. OxyContin, a prescription synthetic narcotic pain reliever nicknamed "Hillbilly Heroin," has made strong inroads in rural areas. So, too, has methamphetamine, a highly addictive drug manufactured from readily available ingredients in rural meth labs. Murders and other serious crimes have rocked small towns swept up in the drug trade.

However, the use of illegal drugs pales in comparison to the abuse of alcohol in rural America. The Muskie School of Public Service at the University of Southern Maine describes substance abuse among rural youth as "A Little Meth and a Lot of Booze." In another study involving an anonymous survey of rural Mississippi middle school students, a shocking 17 percent of students had driven after drinking alcohol and just under half—45 percent—had ridden with a driver who had been drinking. Because so many rural children drive tractors and ATVs at an early age, they're apt to combine drinking with driving even though they're too young to have a license.

- Statistics tell a sobering tale about rural substance abuse: Young adults (eighteen to twenty-five) in the smallest rural areas use methamphetamine and OxyContin at twice the rate of their urban counterparts.
- Children (twelve to seventeen) from the smallest rural areas are more likely to have used alcohol, engaged in binge drinking, and driven under the influence than urban children.
- In south-central Wyoming, more than 30 percent of people under age twenty binge drink—50 percent above the national average, according to federal health statistics.

Getting treatment in rural areas can be a challenge. Treatment centers tend to be few and far between, with little public transportation to get to them. Available facilities often lack the expertise of metropolitan health centers. Also, the culture of rural America emphasizes individualism and self-sufficiency, making it difficult for some people to seek help.

To overcome these barriers, some programs focus on prevention, early intervention, and family support. New Mexico has come up with a particularly novel idea: "talking urinals." These devices, hidden in deodorant blocks, cost $21 each and last three months. The state has installed them in five hundred bars and restaurants throughout the state.

"Hey, big guy," the female voice of the talking urinal says, greeting a visitor to the men's room. "Having a few drinks? Think you had one too many? Then it's time to call a cab or call a sober friend for a ride home."

Whether or not these new devices are effective remains to be seen.

Sociologist Cynthia M. Duncan profiled Gwen Boggs along with two other women—Caroline Gage and Deborah Shannon—in similar circumstances, in her book *Worlds Apart: Why Poverty Persists In Rural America.* Based on the author's extensive interviews, these three composite figures show the role communities play in helping or hurting individuals who want a second chance in life.

Like Gwen, Caroline Gage longed to move past her "messing up" years. One of thirteen children in a poor black Mississippi Delta family riled by domestic violence, she missed so much school because of her family responsibilities that the principal told her to stop coming after eighth grade. To escape a life of drudgery in the fields, she married at the age of fifteen, but soon found her husband was abusive and moved back to her hometown. She had five children out of wedlock and went to work in a sewing factory. Caroline wanted to move to her uncle's farm in Arkansas but didn't have the money.

Deborah Shannon also grew up in a troubled family. The daughter of an alcoholic father who abused her mother, Deborah dropped out of school and ran wild in her old mill town in northern New England. After having a child out of wedlock, she received welfare for four years, then found part-time work in a restaurant, married an old friend, and thought about developing a career.

Of the three women trying to rise out of poverty, Deborah alone succeeded. In Gwen's town in Appalachia and Caroline's in the Mississippi Delta, middle-class residents side with the wealthy coal barons and plantation bosses to keep the poor isolated in separate schools and menial part-time jobs. In Deborah's community in Northern New England, on the other hand, everyone "rubs elbows" with everyone else.

Whereas Gwen's and Caroline's tattered clothes and rough speech set them apart from the mainstream, Deborah blended in. Even though Deborah grew up in a troubled, chaotic family, she developed relationships in school and in the community that gave her a sort of "cultural tool kit" to turn her life around. She got a good education in school and mixed easily with children from the middle class. The communities where Gwen and Caroline lived, on the other hand, gave them few tools for upward mobility.

Deborah eventually married an old classmate from a solid blue-collar family and took steps toward becoming a nurse. Gwen, on the other hand, put her dreams of a teaching career on hold because she lacked the resources and encouragement to go back to school. Similarly, Caroline held out little hope of ever leaving the Mississippi Delta.

Duncan, the author of *Worlds Apart*, found education to be linked to race and class. In the highly stratified communities, the wealthy sent their children to separate, often private, schools and vetoed tax increases to pay for improvements in public education. Administrators who rose to their positions through political patronage let school buildings deteriorate and failed to bring in state and federal resources for educational programs.

In the Mississippi Delta, for instance, whites had little social contact with blacks. Whites enjoyed economic power and security while most blacks were poor and powerless. Patterns established during slavery persisted long after emancipation:

- Around two thirds of whites had a high school degree or more, compared to only one third of blacks.
- Nearly a fifth of whites had completed college, compared to only about four percent of blacks.

"The path out of poverty is remarkably similar across all three communities described here," writes Duncan. "In every case, a good education is the key that unlocks and expands the cultural tool kits of the have-nots, and thus gives them the potential to bring about lasting social change in their persistently poor communities."

7 Homelessness

RUSTY BOOKER WANTED TO RUN AWAY FROM HIS
alcoholic mother and abusive stepfather.

But he didn't know where to go. Although he had been in foster
care for a brief time, the state had returned him to his mother and
stepfather. Rusty called his former foster parents, who told him
about the national Safe Place program. He made his way to the
public library with the Safe Place sign out front. From there, he
went to a YMCA shelter in Louisville, Kentucky.

"I felt safe for the first time in many years," he recalled.

Seventeen-year-old Rusty told his story to members of Congress holding hearings on one of the nation's most vulnerable
populations: homeless youth. In addition to runaways, missing
children, and young people thrown out of their homes, the homeless in America include large populations of:

- the mentally ill;
- substance abusers;
- victims of domestic violence;
- minorities;
- families unable to find affordable housing.

Whatever their circumstances, homeless individuals typically
suffer from feelings of shame and embarrassment. They experience
rates of depression almost twice as high as the general population.

Deinstitutionalization—the process of moving severely mentally ill people out of large state institutions—aimed to provide a

Some states are better organized than others in helping the homeless. Stephen Ricardo, nine, and his family have been getting help from a Florida outreach program. They have been able to live in an assistance center until permanent housing can be found.

more humane and less restrictive form of treatment. The movement began in 1955 with the widespread introduction of chlorpromazine, commonly known as Thorazine, an antipsychotic medication. Since then, more than 90 percent of state psychiatric hospital beds have been eliminated.

Although some discharged patients have successfully made the transition to the community, many others floundered and stopped taking their medication. Civil libertarians have opposed forced hospitalization except in cases where the mentally ill pose a clear danger to themselves or others. With few psychiatric beds left, many of the mentally ill have ended up in general hospitals, nursing homes, prisons, homeless shelters, and on the streets. Individuals with severe mental illness comprise about one third of the homeless population, according to the Treatment Advocacy Center, a national nonprofit advocacy organization dedicated to eliminating legal and clinical barriers to timely psychiatric treatment. Some homeless people turn to substance abuse as a form of self-medication.

Rusty's path from homelessness to college-bound high school student was a bumpy one. He abused drugs and alcohol, fought with foster parents, and landed in jail. Finally, he returned to his first caseworker, who helped put him on the road to success.

Researchers divide the homeless into two groups: the sheltered and the unsheltered. While 56 percent of the homeless live in shelters or transitional housing, the remaining 44 percent are unsheltered. A recent study reports the racial/ethnic composition of the homeless to be 45 percent white, 38 percent African American, 10 percent Hispanic, 5 percent American Indian, and 1 percent Asian.

In terms of household structure, single adults comprise about 59 percent of the homeless population. Families make up the remaining 41 percent, the fastest-growing segment of homeless people. One illness, accident, or missed paycheck can make it impossible for a household to pay the rent.

David and Gina Christian and their four children ended up in transitional housing in Dallas, Texas, after David, thirty-four, lost his job fixing cars. Gina, thirty-six, was a nursing home temporary worker and didn't make enough money to cover the family's expenses. Like Gina, many people unable to find permanent positions take temporary jobs even though they typically fail to provide regular wages and benefits. Before getting help from the Interfaith House in Dallas, David sold tires from their two cars to pay for their nightly meals of beans and rice. In an interview with *Time* magazine, Gina said, "I felt degraded, like I was less than human."

Many apartment-seekers find affordable housing in short supply. The price of housing has risen higher than the salaries of workers in low-income jobs. Old boarding houses and single-room-occupancy hotels have given way to luxury condominiums. Unwilling or unable to go to homeless shelters, many homeless Americans live in their cars, in abandoned buildings, or on the streets.

Criminalizing the Homeless

One cold night in February, Augustine Betancourt tucked himself into his cardboard box and fell asleep on a bench in a small park in

Begging in the Streets

Is begging protected by the First Amendment?

That's the question the courts faced after police in New York City arrested Jennifer Loper and her friend, William Kaye, for loitering in 1992. Loper had moved out of her parents' suburban home to beg on the streets of New York.

In Loper's case, the courts agreed that her right to free speech had been violated because the sidewalks historically served as a public forum. However, in cases of "aggressive panhandling," officials often take a harder line.

Numerous municipalities have passed regulations against aggressive panhandling to prohibit activities such as following passersby after they have refused to give money or intimidating people into giving. In Gretna, Virginia, town leaders passed an emergency ordinance banning aggressive panhandling after residents were wakened at night by beggars banging on their doors. Town Manager David Lilly told *USA Today*, "It's being fueled by the crack industry."

Many experts recommend that conflicts over panhandling be resolved informally rather than taken to court. For instance, municipal leaders might adopt public education campaigns to encourage people to give to charities instead of panhandlers. Some merchants offer panhandlers odd jobs so they won't need to beg outside their stores. And, instead of arresting panhandlers, police officers typically tell them to "move along." Indeed, some officers cultivate panhandlers as informants because they know what is happening in the streets.

New York City. At about 1:30 a.m., two police officers awakened him. It was his first arrest.

"It was the worst day of my life," Betancourt later told the *New York Times*.

Such incidents of "criminalizing the homeless" highlight the difficult questions local officials face when conflicts about public space pit the civil liberties of the unhoused against the rights of the majority. Do residents and merchants who object to homeless individuals urinating and defecating in public have legitimate grounds for police action? How should communities deal with dangers to the public such as tripping over people and objects on the sidewalks, intimidation of passersby caused by aggressive begging, and public discomfort caused by poor personal hygiene? What is the best way to balance compassion for the homeless with the public's rights to clean and safe streets?

For Betancourt, a thirty-three-year-old army veteran who had spiraled into homelessness after his odd jobs tapered off, sleeping on the street had become a way of life. With the help of a lawyer he found in a soup kitchen, he filed a class-action suit against the city for violating his civil rights.

"After you spend a certain amount of time in the streets, as difficult as your circumstances are, they become a routine," Betancourt said in an interview. "You want to avoid disruption of the familiar—even if it's sleeping in an alley."

Although Betancourt lost his nine-year legal battle with the city, he ultimately achieved a measure of victory. His lawyer persuaded him to move into a single-room-occupancy hotel. Betancourt finally sought treatment for his illnesses—major depression and an array of personality and anxiety disorders, including social phobias—that had been undiagnosed for years.

Cases like Betancourt's have found their way to courts throughout the nation, with mixed results. In Los Angeles, for instance, the homeless won a victory by being allowed to sleep on sidewalks as

Some cities have passed laws banning the homeless from their streets. In Los Angeles, sleeping on the streets is legal unless building entrances are blocked. To help solve the problem, the city has invested $12 billion in a plan calling for more affordable housing, shelters, and better services for the poor.

long as they didn't block building entrances. Similarly, in New York a court struck down a ban on panhandling because sidewalks historically had served as public forums. On the other hand, municipal officials in Orlando, Florida, passed an "anti-feeding ordinance" to crack down on churches and activists who had been feeding large groups of homeless people in downtown parks.

Advocates for the homeless argue that the money used to prosecute the homeless could be better spent on programs to help them. In some cities, police sweeps are giving way to outreach work by officers and service providers. Also, policy makers nationwide are working to get the homeless out of temporary shelters and into permanent housing.

Housing the Homeless

Nancy Quinn dragged an old box spring from the garbage to her makeshift home under an overpass in the South Bronx.

Huddled under six blankets, she spoke to a reporter for *New York* magazine about her life as a drug addict, sexual-abuse victim, and prostitute.

"I have no pimp," she told the reporter, giggling. "You want to hear something bad? You want to know who my pimp is? My stem is my pimp. My crack pipe."

A thirty-eight-year-old mother of three, Quinn avoided homeless shelters because they typically required people to stop using drugs or at least to enter a rehab program or get counseling. Several years had passed since Augustine Betancourt was arrested for sleeping in a cardboard box. As mayors had changed in New York, so, too, had policy regarding the homeless.

New research had shown that giving homes to the homeless could actually save money by reducing the costs spent on emergency rooms, shelter beds, jail cells, psychiatric hospitals, and other services. Experts, though, say that living alone can be a challenge, especially for individuals struggling with physical and mental health issues. Support services are crucial, but, even then, not everyone accepts the help. As Nancy's story shows, getting the homeless off the streets and into better lives is no simple matter.

In 2008, outreach workers in New York convinced Quinn to accept a free room in an apartment house about a half mile from the overpass. Reconnecting with her teenage son had shown her how far she had fallen. At first, Quinn reveled in her new home, delighting in the shower and the electricity. But, that same night, she slipped out to smoke crack. She was arrested and charged with a class-A misdemeanor, her thirty-ninth arrest. Once she was released, she returned to her home below the underpass, not the apartment.

She didn't want to smoke in the apartment, but she wasn't ready to get clean either. Instead, she wanted to have it both ways: to have a new life but not to give up her old life.

"I want to get nice and high," she told the reporter. "I need something to eat, and then I can go there and lie down."

8 Jobs

MICHELLE GORDON BOUNCED FROM JOB TO JOB.

A single mother with four children, she worked as a call center employee, a nurse's aide, and a janitorial supervisor, but nothing took. She moved back with her mother and mowed lawns to make ends meet. Michelle described her life since welfare reform as "a little bit of a roller coaster."

Mary Bradford, on the other hand, made a successful transition from welfare to work. Also a single mother, she landed a clerical job that led to a supervisory position in the same company. In a matter of ten years, she doubled her earnings.

These two women, profiled in *USA Today*, illustrate both the successes and the frustrations of welfare reform. Passed in 1996, the Personal Responsibility and Work Opportunity Reconciliation Act aimed to end welfare dependence by promoting education, job training, family responsibility, and work. The act requires recipients, who are mostly single mothers, to work at least part-time after receiving assistance for two years. It puts a five-year lifetime limit on benefits.

Using a carrot-and-stick approach, the Transitional Assistance for Needy Families (TANF) program offers recipients help with child care, job training, and transportation if they work, and sanctions if they don't. States can make exceptions for certain hard-to-employ individuals. The 2006 renewal of the welfare act tightened work requirements.

This young Hispanic woman is participating in a ten-month medical tech program that will prepare her to get off welfare and find a job.

Welfare reform has dramatically reduced caseloads. The number of welfare recipients dropped from 12.2 million in August 1996 to 4.5 million in June 2005, a 64 percent decline. Critics of welfare reform, however, argue that many former recipients end up in low-wage jobs with inadequate child care and health coverage.

Clearly, some individuals in welfare-to-work programs do better than others. Those coming from impoverished neighborhoods where few people hold steady jobs face special challenges, especially if their support systems break down.

"Flat Broke"

Consider the case of Carolyn (not her real name). A once-married, single African-American mother featured in Sharon Hays' book

Flat Broke with Children: Women in the Age of Welfare Reform, Carolyn left her husband after he abused her. The effects of the abuse led to a nervous breakdown requiring hospitalization. Carolyn lost her job and went on welfare.

When her daughter was two, she returned to work. Three years later, her sister was imprisoned for selling drugs. Carolyn took in her three nieces (ages three, nine, and twelve) so they wouldn't end up in foster care. She got a second job to bring in more money and juggled her many responsibilities with the help of her brother and sister-in-law, who assisted with child care and transportation. Then they moved out of town, leaving Carolyn dependent on public transportation and paid caregivers. Next, she got laid off from one of her jobs. Finally, the stress of her situation affected her health, resulting in serious heart problems. Her doctor urged her to "take it easy."

Carolyn returned to her local welfare office. Would she be able to find a program to help her back on her feet? Her future hung in the balance, dependent on the public programs in her geographical area.

Trial and Error

Fred Keller, the head of Cascade Engineering, Inc., in Grand Rapids, Michigan, wanted to help people make the leap from welfare to work. Not only did Keller believe such a move would benefit society, he also thought it could be "good business." In addition to the financial incentives the state offered to participate in its welfare-to-work program, Cascade would get a boost in productivity if it could retain a new corps of dedicated workers. However, Keller found hiring people from poverty much more of a challenge than he had originally expected.

A case study in the *Stanford Social Innovation Review* describes how Cascade's early attempts at hiring welfare-to-work employees failed. During the company's first try, former welfare recipients used a company van to get alcohol and drugs. Next, the company tried partnering with Burger King, offering prospective employees a chance to advance from fast-food to plastics after six months. However, none of the workers stayed at Burger King long enough to make it to Cascade.

Learning from these two failures, Keller decided to try again. This time, everyone at Cascade attended a "Hidden Rules" training based on Dr. Ruby Payne's book *A Framework for Understanding Poverty*. In her book, Payne describes how people live by the rules of their own social class—poor, middle class, or wealthy—which are usually unfamiliar to outsiders.

Keller brought in social workers to work at Cascade. The company had learned from past failures that employees needed more support than they could get from off-site caseworkers with high caseloads. The new staffers helped employees deal with everything from broken-down cars to domestic violence. Instead of punishing a battered employee for being unable to work, Cascade's team told her to take the week off. She returned to work grateful for the support. The company had learned that by making employees feel important and valued it could boost productivity.

"The organization actually is more energized," Keller said. "People are more focused because they know that the organization values everyone there and we actually get more done."

Not all employers, however, go to such lengths to train and retain workers. In many workplaces, employees feel disposable.

"Good Jobs" and "Bad Jobs"

Jeffrey Evans lost his $14.55-an-hour factory job after the plant shut down in the wake of a labor dispute. He searched for a new job but found nothing comparable to his old one. Settling for sporadic construction work, he saw his income cut in half. Forty-nine-year-old Jeffrey moved back with his mother, Shirley Sheline, seventy-three, who had worked at the same auto parts plant.

"Can you believe it, a grown man forced to move back with his mother?" Sheline asked a reporter for the *New York Times*.

Stories such as Evans's have become increasingly common as high-paying manufacturing jobs give way to lower-paying positions in the service sector. Some of the job loss in the manufacturing sector can be blamed on factories moving their plants overseas to take advantage of cheaper labor as a result of free-trade agreements such as NAFTA (North Atlantic Free Trade Association). At the same time, more employers across America have scaled back benefits and made jobs part-time, temporary, or freelance.

Labor unions have long helped workers gain better pay and working conditions from their employers. However, former president Bush's administration curbed the power of unions by weakening enforcement of labor laws. In 2008, after reviewing a sampling

Wal-Mart has brought cheaper goods to consumers, but many workers feel it is at the price of their well-being. These protestors from a group called Jobs with Justice wear hazardous materials protective suits and hand out leaflets protesting their belief that the mega-chain provides unaffordable health care and unlivable wages while engaging in union-busting practices.

of cases brought to the Wage and Hour Division of the Labor Department, the nonpartisan Government Accountability Office reported that the division failed to adequately investigate complaints that workers were not paid the minimum wage, were denied mandatory overtime, or were not paid their last paychecks.

Is a low-wage future inevitable?

Not necessarily, writes Beth Shulman, the author of *The Betrayal of Work: How Low Wage Jobs Fail 30 Million Americans.* Shulman argues that nothing about the jobs themselves makes work in manufacturing "good" and positions in the service sector "bad." As she sees it, the good jobs of tomorrow could be in the service sector. These jobs are growing, and many can't be outsourced. While workers in India might be able to give you technical assistance over the phone for your computer, they're not physically close enough to pour your coffee at the local diner. Whether or not the service jobs of the future can provide the same kind of decent pay as yesterday's manufacturing jobs remains to be seen.

She writes:

> A critical fact is that there is nothing inherent in putting together cars or handling molten steel that makes these jobs "good." In fact, at one time these jobs were hazardous, low-wage jobs that provided few benefits. . . . In exactly the same way, nothing is inherently "bad" about the job of a child-care worker, nursing-home aide, security guard, emergency medical technician, janitor, or hotel worker. It is time we discarded the notion that something in a particular job chains it forever to low pay and miserable conditions.

Shulman offers a three-step solution for boosting the pay of low-wage jobs. First, raise the minimum wage. Second, reward good employers. Third, pave the way for workers to unionize.

Antilabor campaigns by employers have forced many workers into submission. She recommends stiffer penalties for employers who harass, intimidate, or fire workers for their union activities and that these employers be prohibited from receiving public monies. In addition, she calls for new mechanisms to prevent employers from stalling to prevent a contract.

No Health Insurance

Flor Segunda knew nothing would change without a union. After eight years of cleaning lawyers' offices in suburban New Jersey, she still earned only $6 an hour. She received no health insurance. If she got sick, she either lost a day's pay or worked sick.

"We get nothing," she told Shulman. "No health insurance, paid vacation leave, or retirement plan."

Segunda and five of her coworkers sent a letter to their boss asking for a pay raise. Instead, they got fired. The local Service Employees International Union helped Segunda file charges for wrongful dismissal with the National Labor Relations Board. After seven months, she got her job back and began trying to organize her coworkers into a union.

Workers like Segunda who have no health insurance end up relying on the emergency room as their primary care. Some employers offer health insurance plans that require workers to pay the bulk of costs. For example, Wal-Mart's health insurance is so expensive that many employees choose instead to seek public coverage.

Whether employers or the government should pay for health insurance remains a question of much debate. However, everyone agrees that, until something changes, workers will go without health insurance, risking their well-being and that of their children.

A Living Wage

Jamila Mozeb, a twenty-six-year-old single mother of four, couldn't afford to take a day off from work to file for government assistance.

Her $9.50-an-hour job left her having to "rotate" her bills, making partial or late payments. Sometimes she cooked up a big pot of spaghetti and made it last for a week.

However, in the spring of 2007, Mozeb got a new burst of hope. Maryland had passed the nation's first statewide "living-wage" ordinance, following in the footsteps of the many municipalities that had implemented such standards. Maryland's law, which took effect in the fall of 2007, boosted Mozeb's hourly wage to $11.30 an hour.

Mozeb is one of the beneficiaries of more than 130 living-wage ordinances that have won approval across America since Baltimore passed the first such bill in 1994. In addition, twenty-nine states have increased their minimum-wage levels above the federal minimum. A living wage tends to be higher than a minimum wage because it takes into account the real costs of living in a particular geographical area.

Living-wage ordinances vary in their scale and scope. Some are limited to government contractors working on municipal projects. Others extend to all employers in a particular jurisdiction.

Critics of living-wage ordinances argue that they jeopardize employment by prompting employers to leave town rather than pay workers higher wages. However, some community leaders say they'd rather not have such employers anyway.

In particular, "big-box" retailers such as Wal-Mart have come under fire for putting small competitors out of business, turning possible green spaces into vast parking lots, and failing to provide employees with decent wages and benefits. As David Barron, a professor at Harvard Law School, put it: "This surge of interest in regulating big-box retail shows that, at last, American cities are beginning to think of themselves as choosers rather than beggars." Many employees, too, would rather be choosers than beggars.

Moving Up

Piotro (identified by first name only) advanced from a low-wage job bussing tables in a restaurant to a high-paying position as a wine server. The Culinary Training Academy in Las Vegas, Nevada, helped Piotro make the transition from dirty dishes to dapper suits.

Like other successful programs for low-wage workers, the Culinary Training Academy, a collaboration between unions and businesses, gives participants hands-on instruction while they continue to work. Piotro is one of the academy's self-described "success stories."

Piotro's story illustrates how a low-wage job can be a stepping stone rather than a dead end. Certain fields, such as education and health care, lend themselves to such programs because workers are needed at both the entry and professional levels.

María Aragón, for instance, entered a twelve-week training program to be a certified nursing assistant through the Bethel New Life, Inc., program in Chicago. The program allowed her to work and get career training simultaneously. Once she finished her training, she landed a job and began working on her nursing degree at a local community college.

"I believe this education has me off to a good start," she told researchers. "Daily I face the challenge of balancing work, school, studying, and family, but I am not giving up."

Whether the lessons learned from success stories like María's can be applied to the millions of other Americans living in poverty remains to be seen. Poverty is a complex condition in which one setback can set off a chain reaction.

9 Solutions

NO ONE THINKS IT WILL BE EASY.

Poverty has dogged America for centuries. From poorhouses to welfare reform, people have long felt the pinch of not having enough. America is the richest nation on the face of the earth, but one out of eight of us lives below the poverty level.

Still, some progress has been made over the years. The poverty rate among the elderly has declined dramatically as a result of Social Security. Reductions in teenage pregnancy and increases in the number of single parents in the workforce also have brought promising results.

But, experts argue that more can be done. In his book *One Nation, Underprivileged*, author Mark Robert Rank describes poverty in America in terms of two well-known games: Monopoly and Musical Chairs.

First, imagine a game of Monopoly in which the players start out with different amounts of cash and property. This, Rank writes, is like social class in America, which tends to be passed down from generation to generation. Those in the upper echelons have an advantage over everyone else.

Next, Rank likens success in America to a game of Musical Chairs. Without enough decent-paying jobs to go around, not everyone gets a seat at America's table of plenty. A majority of Americans have experienced poverty at some point in their adult lives, according to Rank.

Many people below the poverty line have diabetes, a potentially crippling and very expensive disease. This fourth grade Texas student is being tested for signs of prediabetes with the hope that, if such signs are found, the disease can be halted in its tracks.

As Rank and other experts see it, the nation can harness its long-standing values of work, opportunity, family, and thrift to help build a brighter future for all Americans. The personal responsibility advocated by conservatives and the structural supports championed by liberals need to go hand-in-hand, they say. Because poverty affects all aspects of life, experts recommend a comprehensive approach linking services. Here are some examples of innovative measures that have improved the lives of real people.

Creating New Jobs

During the Greta Depression, FDR's New Deal created millions of jobs in public works. Plans for economic growth in the twenty-first century call for a similar marriage of job creation with infrastructure upgrades. Public investment in roads, bridges, schools, and public buildings could substantially boost employment.

In addition, some other steps to improve jobs and wages include:

- providing income-loss insurance for individuals who lose their jobs and take lower-paying work;
- offering wage subsidies to employers to stimulate job creation;
- developing public-service employment programs;
- creating new green-collar jobs for the environment;
- distributing pay more equitably to reduce the gap between high- and low-wage earners;
- making transportation to work morek affordable and convenient.

Rewarding Hard Work

Sandra Rascon, a health aide and single mother of four, got good news from her tax preparer: she was eligible for a huge tax credit. By filing for the Earned Income Tax Credit (EITC), she'd receive a refund worth nearly two months of her salary.

"You can use the refund for anything. But I was on a strict budget to buy this home," she told the *Los Angeles Times*. "It was my dream. I can't believe I was able to do it. This year, I'm going to use the refund to buy furniture."

The Earned Income Tax Credit has the same effect as a pay raise, although the costs are shouldered by the government rather than the employer. For a head of household earning $7.50 an hour, the EITC effectively raises the wage an additional $3.00 to $10.50 an hour.

However, Rascon, like many workers, missed out on thousands of dollars for years because she didn't know she was eligible. Enacted in 1975, the EITC was significantly expanded in the 1990s. Most benefits go to families with children, but some researchers recommend expanding the EITC to provide for individuals without children.

Providing Access to Good Health Care

When Tamar Guerra made the transition from welfare to work, she lost her Medicaid benefits. She missed the security of being able to go to her old HMO (a health maintenance organization that provides a range of services to members) whenever she or one of her sons got sick.

"If you have a pain in your finger, they send you to a specialist for your finger," she said in *The Missing Class* by Katherine S. Newman and Victor Tan Chen. "They really take care of you until they make sure you receive appropriate attention."

Eventually, Guerra learned about her eligibility for health insurance through the state of New York. She was eager to enroll. However, to apply, she would need to take a day off from her new job in a cosmetics factory, something she was not ready to do because she worried she'd lose her job.

Guerra's experiences are common. A strong connection exists between poverty and poor health for a number of reasons, including high stress, poor nutrition, unhealthy environments, and the high cost of health care.

Nationwide, the state Child Health Insurance Program (CHIP) implemented in 1998 has helped expand health-care coverage for children, but many families do not know how to (or that they can) enroll for the benefits. Streamlining and simplifying the application process could improve access.

In addition, employers could be required to provide a minimum level of health-care coverage for employees. Finally, many experts recommend a system of universal health-care coverage for all Americans.

One key to reducing the pain of poverty is to provide affordable housing. These newly constructed apartments in Rhode Island were built with funds and loans from a variety of state and federal agencies.

Increasing Affordable Housing

Cartina M., a twenty-seven-year-old single parent and department-store clerk not identified by last name, was living in a high-crime neighborhood in Chicago when she learned of her eligibility for a housing voucher program. The voucher enabled her to move to a condominium in Oak Park, a desirable suburb, and cut her commute by one and a half hours a day, according to the Department of Housing and Urban Development.

However, not everyone is so fortunate. Many apartment seekers cannot find landlords willing to accept their vouchers. Nor can they afford to purchase their own homes. Researchers recommend a variety of measures to help, including:

- enforcing antidiscrimination laws to expand housing options for minorities;
- expanding rent-to-buy programs to help low-income renters become home owners;
- eliminating tax write-offs for high-end real estate.

Improving Child Care and Education

Jeremy Walton, a preschool teacher in Milwaukee, Wisconsin, understands the importance of developing young minds.

"The way I look at it," Walton told the *Journal-Sentinel,* "they are the people that are going to be writing my prescriptions. They're going to be teaching my grandchildren. They're going to be protecting my home. They're going to be lawyers and dentists."

Walton teaches in one of the twenty-six states that have recently increased funding for prekindergarten. Researchers cite quality education from an early age as a key ingredient in moving people out of poverty. How can this become more of a reality?

First, experts suggest a more generous system of child-care benefits such as those of European countries. Second, they recommend a number of steps to improve public schools, including more equitable funding, incentives for teaching in troubled districts, smaller classes, increased counseling, and options such as apprenticeship programs. And, finally, at the college level, they point to programs such as former senator John Edwards's "College for Everyone" in Greene County, North Carolina, which provides one year of public college for students willing to work part-time.

Strengthening Families

In Akron, Ohio, two billboards displayed the face of a twenty-five-year-old man wanted for nonpayment of $9,594 in child support. A tip from a family member led to the arrest of Giovanni Diaz for criminal nonsupport.

Such measures reflect increased enforcement of child-support orders. Steady child-support payments can make a significant difference in the ability of single-parent families to avoid poverty.

But, once again, researchers say that more can be done. If, for example, child-support payments were simplified and automatically deducted from paychecks, collection would be more successful. Policies that effectively hold parents financially responsible for their children might also lead to more responsible early sexual behavior.

But what about young fathers with special problems? If, for example, the noncustodial father has resisted legitimate employment, how can the government collect child support?

Programs such as Fathers at Work deal with just such a dilemma. Launched in six sites across the country in 2001, Fathers at Work helps low-income noncustodial fathers (most of whom had committed drug-related offenses) to obtain living-wage jobs and meet their child-support obligations.

Like most of the men in the program, Derrick got into the drug-dealing business for the instant gratification and fast money. Eventually, though, he wearied of the dangers of getting shot or arrested. Derrick enrolled in Fathers at Work while in a halfway house for criminal offenders. Upon completing the program, he moved in with his girlfriend and found a job working under the table (in other words, his income was not reported) for a friend's business.

"I used to think life was a game and that I could try to get the most money I can, but it didn't work out that way," he told researchers. "So now I'm happy, you know what I mean, just working hard for the money because I'm getting paid good. I got big plans. Pretty soon, hopefully by, I'll say like three months, I'll have me a car."

Boosting Savings and Assets

Aurelio Leonel Alvares-Rosales has a $300-a-week job painting houses in the suburbs of Atlanta, Georgia. Because he didn't earn enough money to set aside the minimum balance required at many banks, he used to cash his payroll check at a twenty-four-hour check-cashing outlet that charged a 3 percent fee. But, thanks to a new financial service outlet in his neighborhood, Alvares-Rosales can keep more of his hard-earned income.

New alternative financial institutions have started catering to the estimated 40 million adults in the United States without bank accounts. Wal-Mart, for instance, already operates some 225 in-store MoneyCenters, which offer services such as check cashing, money orders, and money transfers. By the end of 2008, Wal-Mart plans to have MoneyCenters in one thousand locations, a quarter of its stores.

Savings and assets, such as homes, provide a much-needed financial cushion to protect against emergencies. However, setting aside money can be particularly difficult for families already feeling the financial pinch. Matching-grant programs, known as Individual Development Accounts (IDAs), can provide an extra boost. These new programs match private savings with grants from the government, nonprofit organizations, and/or private donors while typically providing financial counseling. Low-interest loans, too, can help. In one case, an immigrant bought a commercial oven to start a home business baking Dominican cakes.

Toward a Brighter Future

Would efforts to fight poverty cost money?

Yes, researchers say, but some of the expenses would ultimately be recouped. By investing in education and health care, less money would be needed for prisons and emergency rooms. America would be spending resources on the "front end" rather than the "back end" of problems.

In public opinion polls, Americans strongly express their desire for a more equitable society. When asked if they would be willing to pay two hundred dollars a year more in taxes to help the poor, 78 percent of Americans said yes. This would amount to $21 billion to support poverty-reduction initiatives.

However, rather than an across-the-board tax increase, taxes could be redistributed to support antipoverty programs, according to Rank. Over the past thirty years, wealthy households and corporations have benefited dramatically from tax cuts. Closing these loopholes, Rank writes, would result in a more equitable distribution of wealth.

Finally, eliminating poverty might sound impossible, but experts say it's not. Change simply requires a public mandate. As Rank writes, eliminating poverty will come from the simple realization that "impoverishment under-privileges us all."

Notes

Introduction

p. 5, "One out of eight . . .": John Edwards, "Conclusion: Ending Poverty in America," in *Ending Poverty in America: How to Restore the American Dream*, ed. John Edwards et al. (Chapel Hill: University of North Carolina at Chapel Hill, 2007), 256.

pp. 5–6, "The Greeks and Romans lived . . .": Andrew Lindsey, "Absolute Poverty vs. Relative Poverty: The Search for Survival." http://www.associatedcontent.com/article/603931/absolute_poverty_vs_relative_poverty.html (accessed September 23, 2008).

p. 6, "Willie, a roofer in his . . .": David K. Shipler, *The Working Poor: Invisible in America* (New York: Alfred A. Knopf, 2004), 37.

p. 7, "'Social capital' to describe . . .": Lincoln Qullian and Rozlyn Redd, "Can Social Capital Explain Persistent Racial Poverty Gaps?" National Poverty Center Working Paper Series, June 2006. http://www.npc.umich.edu/publications/workingpaper06/paper12/working_paper06-12.pdf (accessed September 23, 2008).

p. 7, "By their bootstraps . . .": Jared Bernstein, "Economic Mobility in the United States: How Much Is There and Why Does it Matter?" in *Ending Poverty in America*, 34.

p. 7, "The income gap . . .": Bernstein, "Economic Mobility," in *Ending Poverty in America*, 34–35.

Chapter 1

p. 9, "Three out of five boys . . .": Milton Meltzer, *Poverty in America* (New York: William Morrow & Co., Inc., 1986), 73.

p. 10, "About half of all white immigrants . . .": S. Mintz, "The Origins of New World Slavery, " University of Houston, http://www.digitalhistory.uh.edu (accessed January 2, 2008).

p. 10, "Idly or unprofitably . . .": John Iceland, *Poverty in America: A*

Handbook (Berkeley: University of California Press, 2003), 11–12.

p. 11, "Franklin disapproved of . . .": Marvin Olasky, *The Tragedy of American Compassion* (Washington, DC: Regnery Gateway, 1992), 43.

p. 11, "Colonists drew a firm line . . .": Iceland, 11.

p. 11, "Pauperism is the consequence . . .": Michael B. Katz, *In the Shadow of the Poorhouse: A Social History of Welfare in America* (New York: Basic Books, Inc., 1986), 19.

p. 11, "Of all the causes of pauperism . . .": Katz, *Shadow of the Poorhouse*, 16.

p. 12, "A winter resort for tramps . . .": Katz, *Shadow of the Poorhouse*, 20.

p. 12, "'Horrid little houses' and garbage-strewn streets . . .": Meltzer, *Poverty in America*, 80.

p. 13, "A proponent of women's suffrage . . .": National-Louis University College of Arts & Sciences, "Jane Addams." National-Louis University, http://www.nl.edu/academics/cas/ace/resources/addams.cfm (accessed January 1, 2008).

p. 13, "Praiseworthy before the war . . .": Rodney B. Dreiser, "Jane Addams and the Dream of American Democracy," *Journal of Leisure Research* (Spring 2004): 282+.

p. 14, "A temporary halt in the prosperity . . .": Katz, *Shadow of the Poorhouse*, 163.

p. 14, "'Hoovervilles' out of bitterness . . .": "Surviving the Dust Bowl," *The American Experience*, PBS, March 2, 1998. http://www.pbs.org/wgbh/amex/dustbowl/peopleevents/pandeAMEX05.html (accessed January 3, 2008).

p. 15, "Jobs not the dole . . .": Joyce Bryant, "The Great Depression and New Deal," Yale-New Haven Teachers Institute, http://www.yale.edu/ynhti/curriculum/units/1998/4/98.04.04.x.html (accessed January 3, 2008).

p. 16, "Enduring gratitude of generations . . .": Katz, *Shadow of the Poorhouse*, 228.

p. 16, "Vietnam War grabbed headlines . . .": *Encyclopaedia Britannica Online*, s.v., "Primary Source Document: Lyndon B. Johnson: The War on Poverty," http://www.britannica.com/eb/article-9116920 (accessed January 4, 2008) .

p. 17, "Prompting a 125 percent increase . . .": Charles Murray, *Losing Ground: American Social Policy 1950–1980* (New York: Basic Books, Inc., 1984), 166.

p. 17, "A man in the house . . .": Murray, *Losing Ground*, 157.

p. 18, "Accused of using eighty names . . .": "The Mendacity Index," *Washington Monthly*, September 2003, http://www.washingtonmonthly. com/features/2003/030,mendacity-index.html (accessed September 23, 2008).

p. 18, "Bill Clinton campaigned . . .": Meltzer, *Poverty in America*, 96.

p. 18, "Has the welfare reform . . .": Iceland, *Poverty in America*, 126.

p. 19, "The new regulations raised . . .": Center on Budget and Policy Priorities, "Brief Guide to 2005 TANF Reauthorization Legislation," November 29, 2005, http://www.cbpp.org/4-21-05tanf.pdf (accessed October 7, 2008).

Chapter 2

p. 20, "I counted the kids . . .": Christopher Gale, "Growing Up Poor," *Teen People*, April 1, 2001, 146+.

p. 20, "The poverty line in 2008 . . .": Department of Health and Human Services, Office of the Secretary, "The 2008 HHS Poverty Guidelines," U.S. Department of Health and Human Services, http://aspe.hhs.gov/ poverty/08poverty.shtml (accessed February 20, 2008).

p. 20, "Here's a statistical snapshot . . .": U.S. Census Bureau, "Income Climbs, Poverty Stabilizes, Uninsured Rate Increases," U.S. Department of Commerce, Census Bureau news brief, Aug. 29, 2006, http://www.census. gov/Press-Release/www/releases/archives/income_wealth/007419.html (accessed February 20, 2008).

p. 21, "Each month debt eats . . .": Ron Haskins, Julia B. Isaacs, and Isabel Sawhill, *Getting Ahead or Losing Ground: Economic Mobility in America* (Washington, DC: Brookings Institute, February 2009), http://www. brookings.edu/reports/2008/02_economic_mobility_sawhill.aspx?p=1 (accessed February 26, 2008).

p. 21, "Life doesn't seem fair . . .": Dirk Johnson and Peter Vilbig, "Money Matters: Left Behind Despite the Boom Economy," *New York Times Upfront*, December 13, 1999, 12.

p. 22, "Visit a slum . . .": David K. Shipler, *The Working Poor: Invisible in America* (New York: Alfred A. Knopf, 2004), 9.

p. 23 "The top one percent of American households . . .": Roger Lowenstein, "The Inequality Conundrum," *New York Times Magazine*, June 10, 2007, 11.

p. 23, "I can get very little . . .": Washington Citizen Action, "A State of Hunger: Improving Washington's Food Stamp Program," June 2002, http://www.nwfco.org/06-01-02_WCA_A_State_of_Hunger.pdf (accessed February 18, 2008).

p. 23, "It's like everyone . . .": *New York Times* correspondents, *Class Matters* (New York: Times Books, 2003), 9.

p. 23, "The old system of hereditary . . .": *Class Matters*, 4.

p. 23, "The gap between the rich . . .": *Class Matters*, 19.

p. 24, "The proportion of students . . .": *Class Matters*, 11.

p. 25, "At 3 Guys . . .": *Class Matters*, 122.

p. 26, "Peralta had been fired . . .": *Class Matters*, 130.

p. 26, "Her new position . . .": Katherine S. Newman and Victor Tan Chen, *The Missing Class: Portraits of the New Poor in America* (Boston: Beacon Books, 2007), 1.

p. 26, "Although the 37 million . . .": Newman and Chen, *The Missing Class*, 3–4.

p. 27, "I'm scared . . .": Dianna M. Nanez, "'Don't Ask, Don't Tell' Immigration Era Ending," *The Arizona Republic*, April 24, 2007, http://www.azcentral.com/arizonarepublic/local articles/0424deportation0424.html (accessed February 15, 2008).

p. 28, "Immigrants account for . . .": Steven A. Camarota, "Immigrants in the United States, 2007: A Profile of America's Foreign-Born Population," Center for Immigration Studies, Nov. 2007, http://www.cis.org/articles/2007/back1007.html (accessed February 15, 2008).

p. 28, "It behooves us to remember . . .": Barack Obama, "Floor Statement on Immigration Reform," April 3, 2006, http://obama.senate.gov/speech/060403-floor_statement_3/ (accessed February 15, 2008).

p. 29, "Now that I can see . . .": Newman and Chen, *The Missing Class*, 173–176.

Chapter 3

p. 30, "Take it from someone who . . .": Rebecca Roach, "It Happens to 'Good Girls' Too," About.com: Teen Advice, http://teenadvice.about.com/library/weekly/aa122100a.htm (accessed January 16, 2008).

p. 30, "Thirty-two percent of families . . .": Isabel V. Sawhill and Ron Haskins, "Work and Marriage: The Way to End Poverty and Welfare," (Washington, DC: Brookings Institution, September 2003), http://www.brookings.edu/papers/2003/09childrenfamilies_haskins.aspx (accessed February 5, 2008).

p. 31, "A child born to an unmarried . . .": Barbara Dafoe Whitehead and Marline Pearson, *Making a Love Connection: Teen Relationships, Pregnancy, and Marriage,* The National Campaign to Prevent Teen and Unplanned Pregnancy, 2008, http://www.teenpregnancy.org/resources/reading/pdf/loveconnection2pg.pdf (accessed February 14, 2008).

p. 31, "Blame their pregnancies . . .": Carol Mendez Cassell, "A Hopeful Future: The Path to Helping Teens Avoid Pregnancy and Too-Soon Parenthood," in *Ending Poverty in America: How to Restore the American Dream,* ed. John Edwards et al. (Chapel Hill: University of North Carolina at Chapel Hill, 2007), 209.

p. 31, "Poverty is the single biggest . . .": Cassell, "A Hopeful Future," 205.

p. 31, "In the past decade . . .": Cassell, "A Hopeful Future," 205.

p. 31, "The decline in teen pregnancy . . .": Cassell, "A Hopeful Future," 205.

pp. 31–32, "The so-called 'abstinence wars' . . .": Cassell, "A Hopeful Future," 211.

p. 32, "Students who take a 'virginity pledge' . . .": Cassell, "A Hopeful Future," 211.

p. 33, "You can't sugar coat . . .": Girls Incorporated, "Advisory Board Member Profile," *Annual Report,* 2003, http://www.girlsinc.org/ic/content/girlsinc_annualreport_03.pdf (accessed February 14, 2008).

p. 33, "In 2000, one out of three . . .": Sara McLanahan, "Single Mothers, Fragile Families," in *Ending Poverty in America,* 80.

p. 34, "The Moynihan Report . . .": Sara McLanahan and Gary Sandefur, *Growing Up with a Single Parent: What Hurts, What Helps* (Cambridge, MA: Harvard University Press, 1994), 7.

p. 35, "McLanahan uses the term . . .": McLanahan, "Single Mothers, Fragile Families," 80.

p. 35, "Married parents who are poor . . .": Children's Defense Fund, "Child Poverty in America," Children's Defense Fund, September 2007, http://www.childrensdefensefund.org (accessed February 14, 2008).

p. 36, "The United States ranked twenty-third . . .": "Psychologist Produces the First-ever 'World Map of Happiness,'" *ScienceDaily* (adapted from research done by Adrian White at the University of Leicester), Nov. 14, 2006, http://www.sciencedaily.com/releases/2006/11/061113093726.htm (accessed October 8, 2008).

p. 36, "They have this thing . . .": Bill Weir and Sylvia Johnson, "Denmark:

The Happiest Place on Earth," ABC News, January 8, 2007, http://abcnews.go.com/2020/story?id=4086092&page=1 (accessed September 22, 2008).

p. 36, "From analyzing a number . . .": "Psychologist Produces the First-ever 'World Map of Happiness,'" *ScienceDaily*.

p. 37, "While an American who earns . . .": David Futrella, "Can Money Buy Happiness?" *Money Magazine*, July 8, 2006, http://money.cnn.com/magazines/moneymag/moneymag_archive/2006/08/01/8382225/ (accessed September 23, 2008).

p. 37, "A survey by the University of Chicago's . . .": Futrella, "Can Money Buy Happiness?"

p. 37, "When you're richer . . .": David Leonhardt, "Maybe Money Does Buy Happiness After All, *New York Times*, April 16, 2008. http://www.nytimes.com/2008/04/16/business/16leonhardt.html (accessed September 23, 2008).

p. 38, "Sociologists use the terms . . .": *New York Times* correspondents, *Class Matters* (New York: Times Books, 2003), 230.

p. 38, "Hays found three patterns . . .": Sharon Hays, *Flat Broke With Children: Women in the Age of Welfare Reform* (New York: Oxford University Press, Inc., 2003), 24, 145–146.

p. 39, "Instead of going to college as planned . . .": Hays, *Flat Broke With Children*, 142.

p. 39, "Women who have children . . .": *Class Matters*, 231.

p. 39, "Only 1.4 percent of them marry . . .": *Class Matters*, 231.

p. 40, "In 2006, Congress allocated . . .": Erik Eckholm, "Program Seeks to Fight Poverty by Building Family Ties," *New York Times*, July 20, 2006, http://query.nytimes.com/gst/fullpage.html?res=9F0CE7DE173FF933A15754C0A9609C8B63 (accessed January 15, 2008).

p. 40, "You see, strong marriages . . .": George W. Bush, interviewed by Alex Kotlowitz, *Frontline*, "Let's Get Married," PBS, November 14, 2002, http://www.pbs.org/wgbh/pages/frontline/shows/marriage/etc/script.html (accessed February 14, 2008).

p. 40, "I thought about marrying . . .": Ashaki Hankerson interviewed by Alex Kotlowitz, *Frontline*, November 14, 2002.

Chapter 4

p. 42, "Everyone else seemed . . .": Christopher Gale, "Growing Up Poor," *Teen People*, April 1, 2001, 146+.

p. 42, "Rolling Meadows trailer park . . .": Dirk Johnson and Peter Vilbig, "Money Matters: Left Behind Despite the Boom Economy," *New York Times Upfront*, December 13, 1999, 12.

p. 43, "Inner cities still hold . . .": Peg Tyre and Matthew Phillips, "Poor Among Plenty: For the First Time, Poverty Shifts to the U.S. Suburbs," *Newsweek*, February 12, 2007, 54.

p. 43, "Now we make 60 pounds . . .": Michael Amon, "As LI Economy Slides, the Newly Poor Seek Assistance," *Chicago Tribune*, Feb. 16, 2008, http://www.chicagotribune.com/topic/ny-lipoo0217,0,5319470.story (accessed November 20, 2008).

p. 43, "Some observers call it . . .": Associated Press, "Poverty Shifts to the Suburbs," MSNBC, Dec. 7, 2006, http://www.msnbc.msn.com/id/16077694/ (accessed February 22, 2008).

p. 44, "Finally, Ash remembers . . .": Jay Ash, interview with the author, March 13, 2008.

p. 44, "In our consumer-oriented . . .": William H. Hudnut III, *Halfway to Everywhere: A Portrait of America's First-Tier Suburbs* (Washington, DC: the Urban Land Institute, 2004), 73.

p. 44, "You looked out for . . .": Ash, interview, March 13, 2008.

p. 45, "Twenty years ago . . .": Sarah A. Klein, "Extreme Shopping, Chicago: What Rising Inequality Means for Retailers, *Crain's Chicago Business*, August 28, 2006, 23.

p. 45, "People will find . . .": Anne Field, "Twilight of the Middle Class," *Retail Traffic*, May 1, 2006, http://www.retailtrafficmag.com/mag/retail_twilight_middle_class/index.html (accessed March 20, 2008).

p. 46, "In this ethnically diverse . . .": W. K. Kellogg Foundation, "Chelsea, Massachusetts," Kellogg Leadership for Community Change. http://wkkf.org/Default.aspx?tabid=90&CID=276&ItemID=2760047&NID=2770047&LanguageID=0 (accessed March 13, 2008).

p. 46, "Today it's more difficult . . .": Ash, interview, March 13, 2008.

p. 46, "The two attackers . . .": Leon Lazaroff, "One Town's Struggle to Accept Immigrants: An Influx of Immigrants has Brought Tension—and Violence—to a Long Island Community," *Christian Science Monitor*, July 23, 2003, 3.

p. 47, "Some townspeople have . . .": Eyal Press, "The New Suburban Poverty," *The Nation*, April 23, 2007, http://www.thenation.com/doc/20070423/press (accessed March 4, 2008).

p. 47, "In Farmingville, for instance . . .": Charisse Jones, "Crowded

Houses Gaining Attention in Suburbs," *USA Today*, Jan. 30, 2006, http://www.usatoday.com/news/nation/2006-01-30-overcrowding-suburbs_x.htm?loc=interstitialskip (accessed March 11, 2008).

p. 47, "So finding that balance . . .": Jones, "Crowded Houses."

p. 48, "If you're good enough . . .": Press, "The New Suburban Poverty."

p. 48, "Many observers attribute . . .": Press, "The New Suburban Poverty."

p. 48, "A strong middle class...": Elizabeth Warren, "The Vanishing Middle Class," in *Ending Poverty in America: How to Restore the American Dream*, ed. John Edwards et al. (Chapel Hill: University of North Carolina at Chapel Hill, 2007), 38.

p. 49, "I'm not as happy . . .": Jennifer Bjorhus, Alex Friedrich, and Maryjo Sylwester, "Fighting for the Middle," *Saint Paul (Minnesota) Pioneer Press*, June 23, 2006.

p. 49, "Since the 1970s . . .": Jacob S. Hacker, "The Risky Outlook for Middle-Class America," in *Ending Poverty in America*, 66.

p. 49, "2 million foreclosures . . .": Jeannine Aversa, "Foreclosures to Rise Whoever Wins White House," *USA Today*, July 6, 2008, http://www.usatoday.com/news/politics/election2008/2008-07-06-candidates-housing_N.htm, (accessed October 10, 2008).

p. 49, "It's not just us . . .": Dana Ford, "Tent City in Suburbs is Cost of Home Crisis," Reuters, Dec. 20, 2007, http://www.reuters.com/article/gc03/idUSN1850682120071221 (accessed March 19, 2008).

p. 50, "In recent years, repo rates...": Kevin David, "Repos in Overdrive: As the Economy Grinds its Gears, the Vehicle Repossession Rate is Hitting a Torrid Pace, Keeping Tow Trucks Busy," *Crain's Chicago Business*, July 14, 2003, 3.

p. 50, "It's not a blood . . .": David, "Repos in Overdrive."

p. 50, "We got swindled . . .": Jenn Abelson, "Entering the Repossession Lane," *Boston Globe*, March 7, 2008, http://www.boston.com/business/personalfinance/articles/2008/03/07/entering_the_repossession_lane/ (accessed March 20, 2008).

p. 51, "We don't have anyplace...": Michele Derus, "Evictions Grow Familiar: As Foreclosures Rise, Days Include Unhappy Surprises for Families," *Milwaukee Journal Sentinel*, June 3, 2007.

p. 52, "Warren points to . . .": Warren, "The Vanishing Middle Class," 43–44.

p. 52, "The solutions to poverty…": Warren, "The Vanishing Middle Class," 50.

Chapter 5

p. 53, "In a *Time* magazine poll . . .": David Von Drehle, "The Limits of Race," *Time* (Oct. 20, 2008), 22.

pp. 53–54, "The stereotypes include that blacks . . .": "Survey Links Racial Views to Obama's Polls Numbers," FoxNews.com, Sept. 20, 2008, http://elections.foxnews.com/2008/09/20/survey-links-racial-views-to-obamas-polls-numbers/ (accessed October 13, 2008).

pp. 53–54, "In a speech before the NAACP . . .": CNN, "Obama's Focus is Responsibility in NAACP Speech," CNN.com, July 14, 2008, http://www.cnn.com/2008/POLITICS/07/14/obama.naacp/index.html (accessed November 10, 2008).

p. 55, "You can't land a plane . . .": Bill Cosby and Alvin F. Poussaint, M.D., *Come on People: On the Path from Victims to Victors* (Nashville: Thomas Nelson, Inc., 2007), 7.

p. 55, "Cosby, though, suggests looking . . .": Lynn Elber, "Cosby Reflects on Obama Win, Pundits' 'Huxtable Effect,'" Associated Press, *Daily Hampshire Gazette*, November 13, 2008.

p. 55, "It doesn't matter if you have the right . . .": CNN, "Obama's Focus is Responsibility."

pp. 55–56, "Here are some of the findings . . .": Erik Eckholm, "Plight Deepens for Black Men, Studies Warn," *New York Times*, March 20, 2006, http://www.nytimes.com/2006/03/20/national/20blackmen.html (accessed October 2, 2008).

p. 56, "Although African Americans make up only 13 percent . . .": Drug Policy Alliance Network, "Race and the Drug War," http://www.drugpolicy.org/communities/race (accessed October 2, 2008).

p. 56, "Black homicide victimization rates . . .": Bureau of Justice Statistics, "Homicide Trends in the U.S.: Trends by Race," U.S. Department of Justice. http://www.ojp.usdoj.gov/bjs/pub/pdf/htius.pdf (accessed November 10, 2008).

p. 56, "I'm trying to stop the bloodshed . . .": Bill Cosby, informal speech (book signing by Cosby and Alvin F. Poussaint, University of Massachusetts, Amherst, November 26, 2007).

p. 57, "You can't put your finger . . .": Cosby book signing, November 26, 2007.

p. 57, "I know you're going to . . .": Carlos McBride, interview with the author, March 9, 2008.

p. 57, "I just want to tell you . . .": McBride, interview, March 9, 2008.

p. 60, "Instead of a harsh approach . . .": McBride, interview, March 9, 2008.

p. 60, "She found the neighborhood . . .": Susan Clampet-Lundquist, "HOPE VI Relocation: Moving to New Neighborhoods and Building New Ties," *Housing Policy Debate*, Fannie Mae Foundation, 2004, http://www.fanniemaefoundation.org/programs/hpd/pdf/hpd_1502_Clampet.pdf (accessed March 3, 2008).

p. 60, "The so-called 'underclass' . . .": Brandon Bosworth, "Our Shrinking Underclass," *The American Enterprise* (May 2006), 52.

p. 61, "An effort needs to be made . . .": Clampet-Lundquist, "HOPE VI Relocation."

pp. 60–61, "Neighborhoods with high concentrations . . .": Subcommittee on Income Security and Family Support of the House Committee on Ways and Means, 110th Congress, "Statement of Alan Berube, Fellow, The Brookings Institution," February 13, 2007, http://waysandmeans.house.gov/hearings.asp?formmode=view&id=5452 (accessed March 3, 2008).

p. 61, "Million dollar blocks . . .": Jeninne Lee St. John, "A Road Map to Prevention," *Time*, March 26, 2007, 56.

pp. 61–62, "One resident of a high joblessness neighborhood . . .": William Julius Wilson, "When Work Disappears: New Implications for Race and Urban Poverty in the Global Economy," London School of Economics paper, November 1998, http://ideas.repec.org/p/cep/sticas/17.html (accessed April 4, 2008).

p. 62, "In some schools . . .": Jonathan Alter, "The Other America: An Enduring Shame," *Newsweek*, September 19, 2005, 42.

p. 63, "Geek! Egghead! . . .": Ron Suskind, *A Hope in the Unseen: An American Odyssey from the Inner City to the Ivy League* (New York: Broadway Books, 2005), 3.

p. 63, "Educators call it . . .": Suskind, *A Hope in the Unseen*, 17.

p. 63, "In an article in *New York* magazine . . .": John McWhorter, "Revenge of the Black Nerd," *New York* magazine, November 9, 2008, http://nymag.com/news/intelligencer/52025/ (accessed November 17, 2008).

p. 63, "More than $25,000 . . .": Jonathan Kozol, *The Shame of the Nation: The Restoration of Apartheid Schooling in America* (New York: Crown Publishing Group, 2005), 60.

p. 63, "It's like we're . . .": Kozol, *The Shame of the Nation*, 28.

p. 64, "Safiya possessed an . . .": Katherine S. Newman and Victor Tan Chen, *The Missing Class: Portraits of the New Poor in America* (Boston: Beacon Books), 87.

p. 64, "The conservative African-American justice . . .": Suskind, *A Hope in the Unseen*, 383.

p. 64, "Skin color really doesn't matter . . .": Sandra Sobieraj Westfall and Bill Hewitt, "Barack Obama Makes History!" *People*, November 17, 2008, 62.

Chapter 6

p. 65, "The level of need . . .": Ian Urbina, "In Kentucky's Teeth: Toll of Poverty and Neglect," *New York Times*, December 24, 2007.

p. 65, "Settlements with fewer than . . .": Anita Brown-Graham, "Top-Down Meets Bottom-Up: Local Job Creation in Rural America," in *Ending Poverty in America: How to Restore the American Dream*, ed. John Edwards et al. (Chapel Hill: University of North Carolina at Chapel Hill, 2007), 231.

pp. 65–66, "Statistics paint a bleak . . .": Brown-Graham, "Top-Down Meets Bottom-Up," 230–232.

p. 66, "Another stereotype is that . . .": Mark B. Lapping, "Where Problems Persist: One-Sixth of the Nation Is Rural—and Many Rural Residents Are Needy," *Planning*, October 2007, 12.

p. 67, "Pine Ridge the poorest . . .": "In Indian Country," *The Economist*, July 10, 1999, 25.

p. 67, "According to writer . . .": Stephanie M. Schwartz, "The Arrogance of Ignorance: Hidden Away, Out of Sight and Out of Mind," *Native Village Youth and Education News*, October 15, 2006, http://www.nativevillage.org/Messages%20from%20the%20People/the%20arrogance%20of%20ignorance.htm (accessed April 29, 2008).

pp. 67–68, "More specifically . . .": Schwartz, "The Arrogance of Ignorance."

p. 68, "26 percent of the population . . .": "Teen Suicide Spirals Out of Control; Tribes, Agencies Work to Respond," *Native American Report*, July 2005, 63.

p. 69, "Within five years . . .": William G. Flanagan and James Samuelson, "The New Buffalo—But Who Got the Meat?" *Forbes*, September 8, 1997, 148+.

p. 69, "Under the tribe's profit-sharing . . .": Sarah Kershaw, "Family Behind Foxwoods Loses Hold in Tribe," *New York Times*, June 22, 2007, http://www.nytimes.com/2007/06/22/nyregion/22pequot.html?scp=1&sq=%22Family%20Behind%20Foxwoods%22&st=cse (accessed April 29, 2008).

p. 70, "Of these, fewer than twenty . . .": Tex G Hall, "Indian Leader Cites Poverty and Pleads for Aid," *New York Times*, February 1, 2003.

p. 70, "Being a migrant also . . .": Norma Flores, essay in "On the Border: Migrant Child Labor," *NOW with Bill Moyers*, PBS, May 28, 2004, http://www.pbs.org/now/politics/migrantchildren.html (accessed April 29, 2008).

p. 70, "Migrant workers like Flores . . .": David L. Brown and Louis E. Swanson, eds., *Challenges for Rural American in the Twenty-First Century* (University Park, PA: The Pennsylvania State University, 2003), 68.

p. 70, "Those in other occupations . . .": "On the Border: Migrant Child Labor," *NOW with Bill Moyers*, PBS.

p. 71, "Increased fear and vulnerability . . .": David Bacon, "Bush's Immigration Clampdown Crimped," *The Nation*, August 22, 2007, http://www.thenation.com/doc/20070827/bacon (accessed October 3, 2008).

p. 71, "By her own admission . . .": Cynthia M. Duncan, *Worlds Apart: Why Poverty Persists in Rural America* (New Haven, CT: Yale University Press, 1999), 196.

p. 72, "We're a frontier . . .": Timothy Egan, "Boredom in the West Fuels Binge Drinking," *New York Times*, September 2, 2006, http://www.nytimes.com/2006/09/02/us/02binge.html (accessed April 23, 2008).

p. 72, "OxyContin, a prescription . . .": Mike Fitzgerald, "Hillbilly Heroin," *Belleville (Illinois) News-Democrat*, September 7, 2003, http://www.opiates.com/media/heroin-belleville.html (accessed May 13, 2008).

p. 73, "University of Southern Maine . . .": Muskie School of Public Service, "Substance Abuse Among Rural Youth: A Little Meth and a Lot of Booze," Research & Policy Brief, June 2007, http://muskie.usm.maine.edu/Publications/rural/pb35.pdf (accessed April 23, 2008).

p. 73, "A shocking 17 percent . . .": "Alarming Rate of Drinking and Driving Among Rural Middle Schoolers Found," *Science Daily* (adapted from research done by the University of Georgia), November 2, 2007, http://www.sciencedaily.com/releases/2007/10/071031121528.htm (accessed May 19, 2008).

p. 73, "Children (twelve to seventeen) . . .": Muskie School of Public

Service, "Substance Abuse Among Rural Youth."

p. 73, "In south-central Wyoming . . .": Egan, "Boredom in the West," *New York Times*.

p. 74, "Hey, big guy . . .": "Steady on the Tequila: Drunk Driving in New Mexico," *The Economist*, March 17, 2007, 37.

p. 75, "Everyone 'rubs elbows' with . . .": Duncan, *Worlds Apart*, 180.

pp. 75–76, "Even though Deborah . . .": Duncan, *Worlds Apart*, 189.

p. 76, "Patterns established during slavery . . .": Duncan, *Worlds Apart*, 96.

p. 76, "In every case . . .": Duncan, *Worlds Apart*, 208.

Chapter 7

p. 77, "I felt safe . . .": House Committee on Education and Labor, "Runaway, Homeless, and Missing Children: Perspectives on Helping the Nation's Vulnerable Youth," Washington: U.S. GPO, 2008, 24.

p. 77, "They experience rates of depression . . .": Melissa J. Doak, *Social Welfare: Fighting Poverty and Homelessness* (Detroit: Thomson Gale, 2008), 148.

p. 78, "Since then, more than . . .": E. Fuller Torrey and Mary Zdanowicz, "Why Deinstitutionalization Turned Deadly," *Wall Street Journal*, August 4, 1998, http://www.psychlaws.orgGeralResources/Article2.htm (accessed October 4, 2008).

p. 78, "Individuals with severe mental illness . . .": Treatment Advocacy Center, "Fact Sheet: Homelessness, Incarceration, Episodes of Violence," Treatment Advocacy Center, Arlington, VA, http://www.psychlaws.org/GeneralResources/fact2.htm (accessed November 21, 2008).

p. 79, "While 56 percent . . .": Doak, *Social Welfare*, 99.

p. 79, "A recent study reports . . .": Doak, *Social Welfare*, 101.

p. 79, "In terms of household . . .": Doak, *Social Welfare*, 102.

p. 79, "Families make up . . .": Doak, *Social Welfare*, 102; Joel Stein, "The Real Faces of Homelessness," *Time*, January 20, 2003, 52+.

p. 79, "Gina said, 'I felt . . .": Stein, "Real Faces of Homelessness," 52+.

p. 80, "Town Manager David Lilly . . .": Tracy Loew, "Cities Crack Down on Panhandling, *USA Today*, January 23, 2008.

p. 80, "And, instead of arresting . . .": Michael S. Scott, "Panhandling," Center for Problem Oriented Policing, Guide No. 13 (2002), http://www.popcenter.org/problems/panhandling/ (accessed May 7, 2008).

p. 81, "It was the worst . . .": Nina Bernstein, "A Homeless Man Challenges New York City Crackdowns," *New York Times*, November 22, 1999, http://www.sciencedaily.com/releases/2007/10/071031121528.htm (accessed May 7, 2008).

p. 81, "After you spend . . .": Sewell Chan, "Ex-Homeless Man, Loser in Court, Feels Victorious," *New York Times*, May 29, 2006, http://www.nytimes.com/2006/05/29/nyregion/29homeless.html?scp=1&sq=&st=nyt (accessed May 7, 2008).

p. 82, "On the other hand . . .": Matthew Philips, "OK, Sister, Drop That Sandwich! Cities Fight Panhandling by Outlawing Food Giveaways in Parks," *Newsweek*, November 6, 2006, 58.

p. 83, "I have no pimp . . .": Robert Kolker, "A Night on the Streets," *New York* magazine, March 17, 2008, 34+.

p. 83, "I want to get . . .": Kolker, "A Night on the Streets," 34+.

Chapter 8

p. 84, "Michelle described her life . . .": Richard Wolf, "How Welfare Reform Changed America," *USA Today*, July 18, 2006, http://www.usatoday.com/news/nation/2006-07-17-welfare-reform-cover_x.htm (accessed March 23, 2008).

p. 85, "The number of welfare . . .": Subcommittee on Human Resources, "A Decade Since Welfare Reform: 1996 Welfare Reforms Reduce Welfare Dependence," House Committee on Ways and Means, February 26, 2006, http://waysandmeans.house.gov/media/pdf/welfare/022706welfare.pdf (accessed May 28, 2008).

p. 86, "Her doctor urged . . .": Sharon Hays, *Flat Broke With Children: Women in the Age of Welfare Reform* (New York: Oxford University Press, Inc., 2003), 37.

p. 86, "Not only did Keller . . .": James R. Bradley, "Bridging the Cultures of Business and Poverty: Welfare to Career at Cascade Engineering, Inc.," *Stanford Social Innovation Review*, Spring 2003, 74.

p. 87, "The organization actually . . .": Bradley, "Bridging the Cultures of Business and Poverty," 81.

p. 88, "Can you believe . . .": Erik Eckholm, "Blue-Collar Jobs Disappear, Taking Families' Way of Life Along," *New York Times*, January 16, 2008.

p. 89, "A critical fact is . . .": Beth Shulman, "Making Work Pay," in

Ending Poverty in America: How to Restore the American Dream, ed. John Edwards et al. (Chapel Hill: University of North Carolina at Chapel Hill, 2007), 114–115.

p. 90, "We get nothing . . .": Beth Shulman, *The Betrayal of Work: How Low Wage Jobs Fail 30 Million Americans* (New York: The New Press, 2003), 20.

p. 90, "For example, Wal-Mart's . . .": Shulman, "Making Work Pay," 119.

p. 91, "Maryland's law, which took . . .": Jamie Smith Hopkins, "Families Discuss 'Living Wage,'" *Baltimore Sun*, May 6, 2007 (archived at progressivemaryland.org), http://progressivemaryland.org/files/public/documents/CLIPS-PM-intheNews/2007May-Dec/2007-5-06-bsun-hucker-familiesdiscusslivingwage.pdf (accessed May 28, 2008).

p. 91, "In addition, twenty-nine states . . .": Shulman, "Making Work Pay," 117.

pp. 91–92, "This surge of interest . . .": David Barron, "American Cities Are Starting to Weigh Up the Pros and Cons of 'Big-Box' Retailers," City Mayors.com, August 24, 2006, http://www.citymayors.com/economics/bigbox_retailers.html (accessed May 22, 2008).

p. 92, "Piotro is one of . . .": Culinary Training Academy, "Success Stories," Culinary Training Academy, Las Vegas, Nevada, http://www.theculinaryacademy.org (accessed May 30, 2008).

p. 92, "I believe this education . . .": Bethel New Life, Inc., "Lessons Learned: Community-Based Organizations and Career Ladder Training," November 1999, http://www.bethelnewlife.org (accessed May 20, 2008).

Chapter 9

p. 93, "A majority of Americans . . .": Mark Robert Rank, *One Nation, Underprivileged: Why American Poverty Affects Us All* (New York: Oxford University Press, 2004), 63.

p. 95, "You can use the refund . . .": Kathy M. Kristof, "Making Use of Earned Income Tax Credit," *Los Angeles Times*, February 10, 2008, http://articles.latimes.com/2008/feb/10/business/fi-perfin10 (accessed June 17, 2008)

p. 95, "For a head of household . . .": Rank, *One Nation, Underprivileged*, 201.

p. 96, "If you have a pain . . .": Katherine S. Newman and Victor Tan Chen, *The Missing Class: Portraits of the New Poor in America* (Boston: Beacon Books, 2007). 132.

p. 98, "The voucher enabled her . . .": U.S. Department of Housing and Urban Development, "Success Stories—Welfare to Work Vouchers," (Washington, DC), http://www.hud.gov/offices/pih/programs/hcv/wtw/ppp/success.cfm (accessed June 17, 2008).

p. 98, "The way I look at it . . .": Joel Dresang and Sarah Carr, "Success Depends on an Early Start," *Journal Sentinel*, Milwaukee, WI, March 4, 2006, http://www.jsonline.com (accessed June 16, 2008).

p. 98, "Walton teaches in one . . .": Dresang and Carr, "Success Depends on an Early Start."

p. 99, "A tip from a family member . . .": "Man Wanted for Nonpayment of Child Support Arrested," *Akron (Ohio) Beacon Journal*, February 8, 2006, http://www.ohio.com/news/break_news/15315041.html (accessed November 21, 2008).

pp. 99–100, "I used to think . . .": Lauren J. Kotloff, "Leaving the Street: Young Fathers Move from Hustling to Legitimate Work," Public/Private Ventures, February 2005, http://www.ppv.org/ppv/publications/assets/183_publication.pdf (accessed June 19, 2008).

p. 100, "But, thanks to a new . . .": Anita Hamilton, "Profiting from the Unbanked," *Time*, August 16, 2007, http://www.time.com/time/magazine/article/0,9171,1653666,00.html (accessed June 9, 2008).

p. 100, "By the end of 2008 . . .": Parija B. Kavilanz, "Wal-Mart Expands Low-Cost Banking Services," CNNMoney.com, June 20. 2007, http://money.cnn.com/2007/06020/news/companies/walmart/index.htm (accessed Oct. 9, 2008).

p. 101, "America would be spending . . .": Rank, *One Nation, Underprivileged*, 187.

p. 101, "78 percent of Americans . . .": Rank, *One Nation, Underprivileged*, 240.

p. 101, "As Rank writes . . .": Rank, *One Nation, Underprivileged*, 254.

Further Information

Balkin, Karen, ed. *Poverty: Opposing Viewpoints*. San Diego, CA: Greenhaven Press, 2004.

Ehrenreich, Barbara. *Nickel and Dimed: On (Not) Getting By in America*. Rockland, MA: Wheeler Publishing., 2003.

Haugen, David M., and Matthew J. Box, eds. *Poverty*. San Diego, CA: Greenhaven Press, 2006.

Shepard, Adam. *Scratch Beginnings: Me, $25, and the Search for the American Dream*. Chapel Hill, NC: SB Press, 2007.

Williams, Mary E., ed. *Poverty and the Homeless*. San Diego, CA: Greenhaven Press, 2004.

Bibliography

Alter, Jonathan. "The Other America: An Enduring Shame." *Newsweek*, September 19, 2005, 42.

Berube, Alan, and Elizabeth Kneebone. *Two Steps Back: City and Suburban Poverty Trends 1999–2005.* Washington, DC: Brookings Institution, 2006.

Chipley, Abigail. "The Hidden Face of Hunger." *Vegetarian Times.* June 2001, 64.

Cosby, Bill, and Alvin F. Poussaint. *Come on People: On the Path from Victims to Victors.* Nashville, TN: Thomas Nelson, Inc., 2007.

Dolliver, Mark. "Resenting the Rich: How the Rise of Inequality Fosters a New Culture of Antagonism." *Adweek.* December 17, 2007, 30(3).

Duncan, Cynthia M. *Worlds Apart: Why Poverty Persists in Rural America.* New Haven, CT: Yale University Press, 1999.

Dyson, Michael Eric. *Is Bill Cosby Right? Or Has the Black Middle Class Lost Its Mind?* New York: Basic Civitas Books, 2005.

Edwards, John, Marion Crain, and Arne L. Kalleberg, eds. *Ending Poverty in America: How to Restore the American Dream.* Chapel Hill: University of North Carolina at Chapel Hill, 2007.

Haskins, Ron, Julia B. Isaacs, and Isabel V. Sawhill. *Getting Ahead or Losing Ground: Economic Mobility in America.* Washington, DC: Brookings Institution, 2008.

Hays, Sharon. *Flat Broke With Children: Women in the Age of Welfare Reform.* New York: Oxford University Press, Inc., 2003.

Hudnut, William H. III. *Halfway to Everywhere: A Portrait of America's First-Tier Suburbs.* Washington, DC: Urban Land Institute, 2004.

Iceland, John. *Poverty in America: A Handbook.* Berkeley: University of California Press, 2003.

Johnston, David Cay. "Report Says that the Rich are Getting Richer Faster, Much Faster." *New York Times.* December 15, 2007, C3(L).

Katz, Michael B. *In the Shadow of the Poorhouse.* New York: Basic Books, Inc., 1986.

Kolker, Robert. "A Night on the Streets." *New York* magazine. March 16, 2008, 34+.

Lowenstein, Roger. "The Inequality Conundrum." *New York Times Magazine.* June 10, 2007, 11.

Meltzer, Milton. *Poverty in America.* New York: William Morrow & Co., Inc., 1986.

Newman, Katherine S., and Victor Tan Chen. *The Missing Class: Portraits of the Near Poor in America.* Boston: Beacon Books, 2007.

Payne, Ruby K. *A Framework for Understanding Poverty.* Highlands, TX: aha! Process, Inc., 2005.

Rank, Mark Robert. *One Nation, Underprivileged: Why American Poverty Affects Us All.* New York: Oxford University Press, 2004.

Shipler, David K. *The Working Poor: Invisible in America.* New York: Alfred A. Knopf, 2004.

Shulman, Beth. *The Betrayal of Work: How Low Wage Jobs Fail 30 Million Americans.* New York: The New Press, 2003.

St. John, Jeninne Lee. "A Road Map to Prevention." *Time*, March 26, 2007, 56.

Stein, Joel. "The Real Faces of Homelessness." *Time*, January 20, 2003, 52+.

Tyre, Peg, and Matthew Phillips. "Poor Among Plenty: For the First Time, Poverty Shifts to the U.S. Suburbs." *Newsweek*, February 12, 2007, 54.

Index

Page numbers in **boldface** are illustrations, tables, and charts.

About the Author

JOAN AXELROD-CONTRADA is the author of several books for middle-school and high-school students. She has written about a variety of topics, including women leaders, the Lizzie Borden trial, and colonial America. Her most recent book for Marshall Cavendish Benchmark was *Plessy v. Ferguson: Separate but Unequal* in our Supreme Court Milestones series. The author's work has also appeared in the *Boston Globe* and various other publications. In addition, she teaches a freelance writing course at the University of Massachusetts in Amherst.